Scullin and the Great Depression: The Australian Labor Party and the Federal Platform 1929 -1931

Dr John McSwiney

KDP – AMAZON Press

TTT

https://www.timetotransform.com.au

Title: Scullin and the Great Depression: The Australian Labor Party and the Federal Platform 1929-1931 / Dr John McSwiney, author.

ISBN: 9798639890406

Cover and internal design by Dr John McSwiney

Typeset in Baskerville 12/24

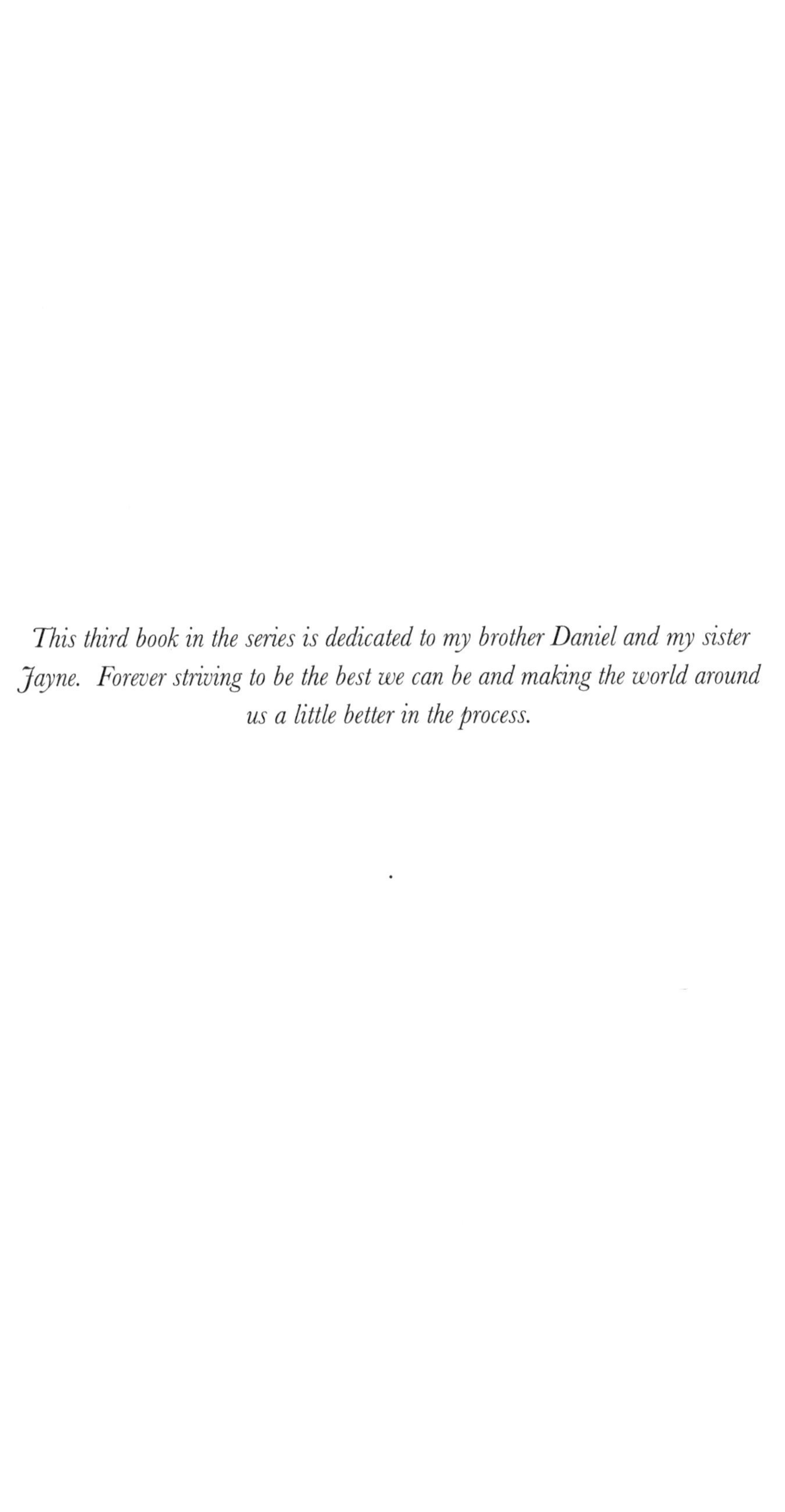

This third book in the series is dedicated to my brother Daniel and my sister Jayne. Forever striving to be the best we can be and making the world around us a little better in the process.

CONTENTS

ACKNOWLEDGMENTS

I am not sure where I got my love of politics but I can still remember the day my father was yelling at the television when Gough Whitlam was sacked: that was interesting!

Thankyou to my parents for instilling in me the value of labour and the importance of standing up for your rights.

Thankyou to my family for loving my eccentricities and putting up with me, including my antics on election day and the ritual watching of the human psephologist Antony Green on the ABC and the theatre of him drilling into the minutia, booth by booth and seat by seat! Love it!

Thankyou to my political heroes growing up, the Hon. Bob Hawke; the Hon. Paul Keating and the Hon. John Cain. All men of vision who understood the importance of the big picture as well as representing working men and women in Australia.

Thankyou to my university professors who entertained me over many years with a myriad of stories and anecdotes and who were passionate about politics, its role in society and the greater good that could be achieved through it. The three most notable and influential were Dennis Woodward; Brian Costar and Derek Verrall. I am indebted to all of you.

Thankyou to all my friends in politics and the trade union movement who I journeyed with for many years. Always fighting the good fight and never giving up. It has been great to be a part of and has provided me with countless memories and many smiles.

1 INTRODUCTION

Book three in the Labor and the Platform series analyses the Scullin government's attempts to enact the platform against a backdrop of rising unemployment, internal party schism and revolt as well of the disintegration of the government over financial and economic policy initiatives instigated to combat Australia's parlous economic state brought about by the Great Depression . Scullin came to power at a time of world peace, but governed during a time of international financial and economic crisis. Also, at no stage during Scullin's administration did he control the Senate and although a number of attempts were made to pursue and enact the platform, nearly every major policy initiative based on the platform was literally destroyed and rendered inoperable by a recalcitrant Senate.

On 11 September 1929 the conservative Prime Minister Stanley Bruce spoke with the Governor General and obtained dissolution of the Parliament[1] and a federal poll was set for 12 October 1929. Labor campaigned extensively during the campaign on maintaining the system of federal arbitration that had developed in Australia in line with stated Labor platform policy since 1901, arguing that the system of federal arbitration was the foundation upon which industrial standards were set and maintained. Labor acknowledged that the federal arbitration system had defects but

---

[1] *C.P.D.*, Vol. 121, 11 September 1929, pp.867-8.

that any shortcomings could be remedied by legislative amendment and not by the wholesale dismantling of the entire system.[2] In fact, during the campaign, the Deputy Labor Leader E.G. 'Ted' Theodore:

> … promised that the mines would be open in a fortnight if his party was successful'.[3]

The Nationalists on the other hand campaigned against the system of federal arbitration and regarded the system as an anathema to the proper functioning of the entire industrial system and sought a mandate to abolish it outright.[4] On 12 October 1929 Australia went to the polls and for the first time in thirteen years, the result was a landslide victory to Labor. Labor candidates were successful in forty-six of the seventy-five seats in the House. Bruce's Nationalists won twenty-four seats whilst the Country Party led by Page won only ten and the remaining five seats were won by Independents, one of whom was the old Labor Prime Minister Hughes who regained his seat of Wentworth principally due to Labor not running a candidate against him.[5] Labor had won fifteen more seats than it had in the 1928 federal election. Labor now held power, however the 1929 federal election was only conducted for the House, there was no concurrent Senate election and the situation remained unchanged in that chamber with seven Labor, twenty-four Nationalist and five Country Party members.

The party makeup in the Senate would bring little comfort to

---

[2] see; Scullin's campaign speech in Richmond on 19 September 1929; *Argus*, 20 September 1929.

[3] *Sydney Morning Herald*, 7 October 1929.

[4] see; Bruce's policy speech in Dandenong on 18 September 1929 and Page's pronouncement in Grafton on 23 September 1929.

[5] The five Government MPs who crossed the floor to bring down the Government: Hughes, Marks and Maxwell from the Nationalists and Stewart and McWilliams from the Country Independents, were given immunity 'from Labor opposition in their respective seats.

Labor for although they had won the election they faced an overwhelmingly hostile Senate and any attempt to enact the platform would have to run the gauntlet through that chamber. However, despite the daunting task facing Labor in the Senate, the biggest surprise of the election was the defeat of Prime Minister Bruce in his seat of Flinders by Labor's Ted Holloway, the Secretary of the Melbourne Trades Hall Council. Commenting on his famous victory Holloway stated:

> The campaign in Flinders was strenuous in the extreme … the electorate … was anything but a Labor seat. But many of its electors were on this occasion aroused by the growing unemployment and the government's industrial, financial and fiscal policies … When after two or three days, all the votes were in and counted, I had the tiniest lead of 60 over the Prime Minister of first preference votes in a poll of 63000. I received the majority (of the independent candidate's preferences) and word was all over Australia that the Prime Minister had been defeated by the Secretary of the Melbourne Trades Hall Council by 305 votes. He [Bruce] had pulled his safe seat from under himself by the wilfulness and overbearing class bias of his policies. I was fully conscious that the Flinders vote *against* Bruce and *for* Labor: E.J. Holloway just happened to have been the man endorsed by Labor.[6]

Holloway's victory provided a positive air to the result for Labor and certainly contributed to the exuberant renditions of the *Red Flag* that were sung in the Hotel Kurrajong by Labor members and supporters who had gathered in Canberra for the start of the new parliamentary session. When Labor assumed office the platform was a little over two years old, having been ratified by Federal

---

[6] Holloway, E. J., From Labour Council to Privy Council. Unpublished Autobiography as cited in Faulkner, 2001, op cit., p.58.

Conference delegates in May 1927.[7] The platform may have been dated but Scullin was in a similar position to Fisher in 1910 when the latter also adopted a platform nearly 2 years old when first entering office. However, any similarities between Fisher and Scullin would end at this juncture. In May 1927 when Conference debated the platform, the Australian economy was buoyant, however in 1929 when Scullin assumed office, the financial and economic landscape of Australia had changed markedly and any lingering mirth held by Labor about the election victory and Labor's ability to pursue and implement the platform would be short lived as Scullin, now in control of the Treasury, was provided with a somber picture of Australia's finances, with the Melbourne *Age* reporting:

> An inheritance of financial complexities also confronts Labor Ministers. The Bruce-Page Government heavily increased public debts abroad, and our external interest obligations now amount to about £30,000,000 a year ... At the same time adverse trading balances aggravated the position.[8]

---

[7] see; Appendix 1 - Australian Labor Party Federal Platform 1927
[8] *The Age*, Melbourne, 15 October 1929.

2 THE ONSET OF THE GREAT DEPRESSION

Scullin took office with the Australian economy in a parlous state due in large part to the policy prescriptions of the Bruce Administration, who from 1926-1929 secured no fewer than nineteen overseas loans primarily with financial institutions in London and New York. In essence, Labor had inherited a crippling budget deficit that was exacerbated by a slump in world commodity prices, the effect of which impacted on Australia's exports of wool and wheat that in turn fed a burgeoning balance of payments crisis. Also, a little over two weeks after Labor won office there were two major financial events that impacted upon Australia, the first was the spectacular collapse of the New York stock exchange and the second was when loan underwriters in London were left with over 80 percent of the Australian issue on their books; the effect being that London loan monies literally dried up overnight leaving an outstanding debt of nearly £35 million to be settled.[9] The combined effect of these events would prove disastrous for the new government, however Labor supporters may have been somewhat buoyed by the analysis of the situation by the *Sydney Morning Herald*:

> The crash cannot but have ramifications far away from the United States, and in the main they may be favourable to

---

[9] During the period July 1929 to February 1930 almost £17 million of Australian gold was shipped to London to cover the debt.

other countries rather than unfavourable. One consequence should be that money will become cheaper … London has already experienced a rise in the value of sterling as against dollars. Loan operations in London should be facilitated, and because of that the tendency should be for Australia to benefit rather than suffer from what has been happening since Thursday last.[10]

The commentary in the *Sydney Morning Herald* had not taken into account the comments of noted economist J.B Brigden[11] who in September 1929 addressed the Constitutional Association of New South Wales and predicted that:

> The national income of Australia will be reduced by at least £30,000,000 and that the indirect loss will be another £30,000,000.[12]

Brigden was unable to provide a definite analysis on the impact of the reduction of national income on domestic production but provided a prophetic scenario that:

> Distributors [trade and transport] would suffer first, and as they gain between one-third and one-half of the overseas price, the loss from this cause in Australia could not be less than £13 millions. This £13 millions is now spent largely on Australian goods and services, and its loss would have cumulative effects throughout Australian industry.[13]

In concluding his speech he stated that:

---

[10] *Sydney Morning Herald*, 31 October 1929.
[11] J.B. Brigden was an economist to the Overseas Transport Association.
[12] *Sydney Morning Herald*, 29 September 1929.
[13] 'Notes on the Economic Position of Australia, October 1929'. *Brigden Papers*, NLA, 21/5/163.

> The worst thing that could happen to Australian industry at
> the present juncture is that the attention of the people
> should be diverted from the real problem by a series of
> political wrangles.[14]

The 'political wrangle' Brigden was referring to was the federal
election that had been called after the Government's defeat on the
Maritime Industries Bill. However, Brigden's warning went
unheeded and the people's attention was transfixed on the election
and not on the economic state of the country. The Scullin
government was elected at a time when London loan monies were
almost impossible to obtain and Wall street had collapsed. The
result being that there was an almost immediate reduction of
capital inflow into the country that adversely affected the
government's ability to pursue the platform and embark on big
spending programs such as capital and public works programs, the
very programs the government wanted to pursue to reduce
unemployment.[15] On 13 November 1929 new Treasurer
Theodore, explained Australia's financial position to Caucus,[16]
whilst according to Robertson, Scullin who had received a private
briefing from the head of the Commonwealth Bank, Sir Robert
Gibson, was 'staggered' to learn the true nature of Australia's
financial predicament.[17] On 21 November, a week after outlining
Australia's predicament to Caucus, Theodore informed the House
of Australia's financial position stating:

> Since the new government assumed office there has not been
> sufficient time to call for fresh estimates in detail from all
> departments ... therefore, the major portion of the Estimates of

---

[14] ibid.

[15] See; *C.P.D.*, Vol. 121, 10 September 1929, p.866.

[16] *Caucus Minutes*, 13 November 1929.

[17] Robertson, J., <u>J.H. Scullin. A Political Biography</u>. University Western
Australia Press, Perth, 1974, p.185.

the late Government has been adopted.

It was the duty, however, of the new Government to examine the Estimates and revise and amend them so far as was necessary to disclose the true position of the Commonwealth finances. This examination revealed that in some important instances the late government had greatly understated the expenditure requirements and over-estimated the probable revenue. The late Treasurer has grossly miscalculated both the cost of the definite commitments of the departments and services for the year, and also the probable revenue.

It is now apparent that if the actual requirements of the year had been provided for in connexion with war pensions, repatriation, other war services, old age pensions, iron and steel products bounty, prospecting for oil and sundry other items ... the estimates of expenditure should have been increased by approximately £500,000 ... [also] customs and excise revenue, land tax and income tax, and other receipts would have fallen short of the estimate by at least £1,050,000. The late Treasurer would, therefore, have finished the year with a deficit of about £1,200,000, instead of a surplus of £360,000, as promised by him in his budget speech. [18]

Theodore's and Labor's plan to tackle the impending deficit was to simultaneously raise revenue by increasing customs and excise duties[19] and income taxes as well as making severe cutbacks in defence expenditure[20] by £150,000 for the year.[21] The monetary

---

[18] *C.P.D.*, Vol. 122, 21 November 1929, p.111.
[19] Increases were mainly imposed on luxury items as set out in the *Tariff Schedule (No 2) Act* 1929, <u>ibid.</u>, pp.120-151.
[20] Compulsory military service and training was abolished.
[21] For an overview of the breakdown of the estimates in defence expenditure,

position of the government, with respect to Labor's ability to raise loan capital for public works expenditure to pursue the platform, was literally under siege and was duly acknowledged by Theodore when he stated:

> Owing to the continuation of adverse monetary conditions in Australia and abroad, the Australian Loan Council has found it necessary to curtail drastically the public works programs of the Commonwealth and State Governments for the present year.[22]

The monetary and budgetary impediments facing the country were decidedly bleak and any advances by Labor in pursuit of the platform would be severely hampered by the deteriorating financial situation. The financial sector was under siege and Theodore then provided an overview of the market in Australia stating:

> The decline in the prices of our principal primary products, combined with diminished production owing to adverse seasonal conditions in certain parts of Australia, has resulted in a considerable reduction of the national income with its inevitable effects on the amount of money available for investment in Government loans. It is unfortunate that coincident with adverse seasonal conditions and business depression in Australia, financial conditions overseas should be so stringent.[23]

Theodore's grim assessment meant that Australia was hamstrung in its ability to raise capital overseas for implementation of Labor's platform. It was at this point that the Government turned to the Commonwealth Bank for assistance and Theodore informed the

---

see: *C.P.D.*, Vol. 122, 21 November 1929, pp.112-113.

[22] ibid., p.114.

[23] ibid.

House:

> When the Government assumed office it was faced with a
> depleted treasury and the necessity of raising an immediate
> loan for the needs of the Commonwealth and the States ...
> the Government met with the chief officers of the
> Commonwealth Bank ... as a direct outcome of the
> discussion, the Treasury immediately issued in Australia a
> loan of £10,000,000.[24]

The Commonwealth Bank provided the government with
temporary finance[25], and although the £10,000,000 was well
received, it was not nearly enough to provide Labor with the
necessary capital to pursue stated platform policy initiatives.
Theodore had elucidated the government's, and the country's,
economic predicament with clarity as well as providing an
overview of how the government was going to address the current
economic downturn, and although Theodore may have been
aware of the perils facing the Australian economy he was not
forthcoming about them when he concluded his budget speech
stating:

> I think it will be generally realised that the new
> Government has assumed control at a period of extreme
> difficulty. We inherited an empty treasury, and an
> impaired credit at home and abroad. However, we do not
> view the future with alarm or pessimism. Australia has
> wonderful recuperative powers, and a stout hearted
> industrious community. If we are blessed with good
> seasons, our troubles will soon disappear, and we shall
> commence a new era of progress and prosperity.[26]

---

[24] ibid., p.115
[25] Gibson informed the Cabinet that the Commonwealth Bank would only
finance the government for five weeks!

Despite Theodore's rhetoric that the country's troubles would 'soon disappear', Australia's underlying economic base was in a parlous state and quite incapable of mounting a serious challenge to combat the Depression that was just about to engulf it and according to Schedvin:

> Despite this re-assessment of the estimates, Theodore's Budget was still grossly optimistic … He and his government had not yet come to grips with the fact that a substantial fall in national income was inevitable even if commodity prices and loan markets improved immediately; nor were they aware of the effect this fall would have on the demand for imports and hence for customs collection.[27]

Theodore's gloss might have distracted some of his colleagues away from the economic tidal wave that was about to hit the country but not all Labor members shared Theodore's positive economic prognostications. The most vocal and arguably the only Labor member who had a portent of just how bad things might become was Frank Anstey who according to Chifley:

> [Anstey] … believed in 1929 that economic conditions in Australia might get much worse for all, and especially for the working classes, before they could conceivably get better. He warned his colleagues that if they refused to challenge and drifted along subject at every move to the veto of the Senate majority, their futility in the face of economic difficulties could quickly lose them the goodwill of the majority … and in all probability would deliver them into the hands of their enemies.[28]

---

[26] *C.P.D.*, Vol.122, 21 November 1929, p119.
[27] Schedvin, C.B., <u>Australia and the Great Depression.</u> Sydney University Press, 1970, p.122.
[28] Crisp, 1977, <u>op cit</u>., p.43.

Similarly, when Gibson informed Cabinet that:

> ... unless the Government indicated how it would reduce expenditure, the Commonwealth Bank could not finance it [the Government] beyond the end of November – five weeks hence.[29]

Anstey was the only member to argue the point with Gibson, who in later years recalled the exchange:

> I suggested he should have said so to the Bruce government twelve months earlier and he replied he had done so. I said:

> The only evidence we have is that you financed Bruce so long as he remained in office and close down on us as soon as we become a government.

> That was promptly resented and I suggested his resentment did not alter the facts. I reminded him that only a few weeks before the elections he had issued a bank report saying there was no justification for pessimism and that general conditions were as good as at the end of 1928. He replied that he had not attended the Cabinet to be cross-examined and insulted and on behalf of the Government Prime Minister Scullin apologised for my rudeness.[30]

Anstey appeared to be the only member of Cabinet (and Caucus), at this time, who fully understood the enormity of not only the economic burden facing Australia, but also the political manoeuvring required for Labor to have any chance of surviving the impending economic collapse that would occur. To Anstey,

---

[29] Ross, op cit., p.104.
[30] Frank Anstey: Memoirs of the Scullin Labor Government, 1929-1932. *Historical Studies*, Vol. 18, No. 72, April 1979, p.368.

Gibson's message was clear and unequivocal and to his mind there was only one logical course for the party to take, it had to find an issue and force a double dissolution, as there was little chance that Labor could effectively pursue its platform:

> When Sir Robert Gibson departed I said: That puts the lid on us. We are going to be blockaded not only by a hostile Senate but by a hostile Bank Board. There is only one way to save our lives – force a double dissolution before the tide of popularity runs from under us.[31]

Anstey advocated forcing a double dissolution 'on any subject the government deemed best' and suggested that Labor pursue plank 1 of the Finance and Taxation section of the platform stating:

> We opposed the farming out of the Commonwealth Bank to private overlords and we pledged ourselves to bring their rule to an end – make that an issue.[32]

Anstey was told by his Cabinet colleagues that they would:

> … do it some saner way than you suggest … [Anstey responded] … I hope so – any sane way will do me.[33]

Unfortunately for Anstey and for Labor the double dissolution trigger was never utilised and the government set about attempting to come to terms with the stark reality that given the economic plight of the country coupled with the situation in the Senate, any attempts by Labor to enact the platform would be extremely difficult, if not impossible.[34]

---

[31] ibid.
[32] ibid.
[33] ibid., p.369.
[34] The Scullin government held office from October 1929 to December 1931, it sat through five separate parliamentary sessions and enacted one hundred and forty-eight Acts (The *Commonwealth Debt Conversion Act* (No. 2) 1931 was printed as

'No. 1 of 1932') of which thirty three were standard financial measures, whilst thirty were minor amendments to existing legislation.

3 GOVERNING IN AN ECONOMIC AVALANCHE

Scullin's first parliamentary session was relatively short with the Parliament only sitting from 20 November 1929 – 13 December 1929. [35] In the first parliamentary session the government managed to secure the passage of thirteen pieces of legislation and of these thirteen Acts the government only managed to pass three Acts of minor significance to the platform. The three Acts were the *Arbitration (Public Service) Act* 1929; *Commonwealth Bank Act* 1929; *Income Tax Act* 1929. All three Acts made minor consequential amendments to their principal Acts and were not based on platform policy.

The first parliamentary session was short, however even in comparison with Fisher's first session of his second government of 1910, it was apparent that Scullin's administration would find it extremely difficult to successfully pursue the platform, as any platform based policy initiatives would have to run the gauntlet of the worsening economic climate as well as the Senate, who up until this stage had not flexed its muscle.

<u>Second Parliamentary Session</u>

In the second parliamentary session[36] the Government secured the

---

[35] See, *C.P.D.*, Vol.122, 1929.

[36] Scullin's second session was again relatively short sitting from 12 March 1930 – 2 May 1930.

passage of fifty-five pieces of legislation and of these fifty-five Acts, eighteen were *Sales Tax* or *Sales Tax Assessment Acts*.[37] These Sales Tax Acts were subdivided into nine groups on the advice of E.M. Mitchell and H.V. Evatt, K.Cs and introduced by Labor in order to avoid infringing section 55 of the Constitution that required Tax Acts to deal with only one subject of taxation. According to Sawer:

> … different Acts dealt with sales direct by manufacturers to the public, sales to the public by purchasers from manufacturers, by importers and so on. Exemptions were designed to avoid raising the cost of exports, and basic foods, and to prevent further taxes on goods already subject to heavy excise duties.[38]

In fact, the new Sales Tax Acts were utilised by the government as part of its wider fiscal policy to combat the deepening depression to the extent that by the end of the Scullin Government reign in 1931 they had enacted a total of forty six separate *Sales Tax Acts*.

Graduated Land Tax

The government's focus was clearly on the worsening depression, however Labor did manage to successfully strengthen plank 2 of the 'Finance and Taxation' section of the platform with the passage of the *Land Tax Assessment Act* 1930 and the *Land Tax Assessment (No.2) Act* 1930.[39] The Land Tax legislation was a positive step by Labor to strengthen an established platform plank. The legislation was significant as it was the only Act passed by Labor during the second parliamentary session related to the platform. However, in the economic and political context in which the Scullin administration found itself it would be negligent to measure the

---

[37] see; *C.P.D.*, Vol. 123, 1930, p.ix.
[38] Sawer, op cit., p.11.
[39] see; *C.P.D.*, Vol. 123, 19 March 1930, pp.211-247 and Senate, 20 March 1930, pp.283-310.

success or otherwise of the government on the legislation it successfully passed through the Parliament, especially given the economic state of the country and the balance of power in the Senate.

Labor had been in office a little over six months and although being continually battered by the worsening effects of the Depression, almost on a daily basis, it had found it difficult to actively pursue the platform in the same manner as Fisher during his first six months in 1910. Labor had grappled with the economic malaise that confronted them, but had taken a cautious approach to dealing with the situation. However, after spending six months coming to terms with the impact of the Depression, Labor began to actively pursue the platform in the belief that pursuing platform initiatives would provide the necessary policy mix required to alleviate the problems facing Australia.

<u>Constitution Alteration Initiatives – Power of Amendment (of the Constitution), Industrial Powers and Trade and Commerce</u>

On 5 March 1930 Scullin submitted two referenda Bills to Caucus for consideration. The first was the Constitution Alteration (Power of Amendment) Bill and the second was the Constitution Alteration (Industrial Powers) Bill. Scullin had reached a point where he knew that he had to be proactive if he was to lead Australia out of the Depression. In the context of the time the Bills were arguably the most far reaching reforms ever to be introduced in the Parliament. The Constitution Alteration (Power of Amendment) Bill was an important measure for Labor and its pursuit of the entire platform. The Bill, if passed, would provide Labor and future governments with the ability to alter the Constitution by obtaining an absolute majority in both Houses. The initiative was crucial to Labor enacting key parts of the platform especially in relation to planks 3, 4 and 15 of the fighting platform, and related

general platform planks, dealing with the nationalisation of 'banking and insurance', 'monopolies', and establishing a 'National monopoly of Assurance, including sick, accident, life and unemployment'; as well as planks 5 of the fighting platform, and related general platform planks, dealing with Arbitration Act amendments. The proposal would be critical to Labor's ability to pursue the platform and combat the Depression.[40]   Caucus members were provided with confidential drafts of the proposals and after discussing the Bills they were subsequently approved and then placed on Labor's parliamentary Agenda for the autumn parliamentary session. Scullin and the Caucus were aware that the Bills would invariably come under siege in the Senate and in all probability would be defeated there, however the Bills would also provide a trigger for the calling of a double dissolution election and provide Labor with an opportunity to win back control of the Senate, thus enabling the Government to pursue expansionist economic policies in line with stated Labor policy and platform.

On 14 March 1930 Scullin introduced the proposals into the Parliament and successfully sought leave of the Speaker to debate both Bills simultaneously as they were, ' … closely related in many ways.'[41] Scullin outlined the rationale for the legislation providing a history of the development of the Constitution including the fact that the constitution was fundamentally flawed:

> The object of the Bill is to confer full power upon this Parliament to amend the Constitution … Very early in the life of the federation, Parliament discovered the weakness of the Constitution … A change in the personnel of the High Court may mean a different interpretation of the Constitution, and an alteration of the powers of this Parliament … Thus, what ought to be a political matter

---

[40] See Appendix 2 – Scullin's Constitution Alteration Proposals
[41] *C.P.D.*, Vol 123, 14 March 1930, p.177.

becomes a judicial one. That is surely not in the interests of democratic government. Important issues like this should be decided, not by courts, but by the Parliament that represents the people. This evil is accentuated by the difficulty met with trying to amend the Constitution.[42]

Scullin also outlined previous attempts by Labor to amend the Constitution, providing a continuity of argument that Labor administrations are forced to amend the Constitution to pursue basic planks of Labor's platform because the official political structures within which Labor operate are arrayed against them:

> The Labor party went to the country in 1910, declaring in favour of the new protection once more, and definitely advocating enlarged powers under the Constitution. A Labor Government was elected with a majority in both Houses, and referred them to the country, but the proposals were rejected by a majority of 248,000 votes. When the 1913 election took place the Fisher Government, undaunted, again submitted similar proposals to the electors, and on that occasion they were defeated by the small margin of 26000 votes. Now seventeen years later, we are again proposing to submit proposals for enlarged powers to the people. During all these years there has been litigation as to the powers of this Parliament, powers that it wishes to put into operation to give effect to the will of the people expressed at general elections. We have had litigation, legal expense, and, worst of all delays, caused by argument not the merits of the propositions submitted but merely on legal technicalities.[43]

Scullin had provided a reasoned argument for the support of the

---

[42] ibid., pp.177-180.
[43] ibid., p.179.

measure and then outlined to the House the checks and balances of the new system if it was successful:

> The only restrictions that are placed upon the power of the Commonwealth to amend the Constitution are contained in the first eight sections. Those sections contain implications which presume a federal system, although they are not very clearly set out … This amendment would enable Parliament, by an absolute majority in each House, to amend the Constitution, but until Parliament passed the necessary legislation the Commonwealth legislative power will remain as it is. The Constitution however, would be more flexible, and the methods of altering it easier and less costly.[44]

Scullin outlined the case for the adoption of the proposal and then he turned his attention towards the provisions contained in the Constitution Alteration (Industrial Powers) Bill. Scullin was quick to go on the offensive immediately attacking the recalcitrant nature of the previous Bruce administration over their handling of industrial arbitration:

> The late Government intended to abolish Commonwealth conciliation and arbitration … The failure of the late Government to honour promise has made it necessary for us to appeal to the people for increased power … If this Parliament is given increased powers over industrial matters we shall be able to improve the present arbitration system … We are asking that this Parliament be given power to amend the Constitution along the lines of the election programs submitted to the people.[45]

---

[44] ibid., pp.183-4.
[45] ibid., pp.184-5.

Industrial arbitration was central to Labor's election manifesto and a key plank in the fighting and general platforms. Labor had been elected with an electoral mandate on the issue, however the economic crisis had overtaken industrial matters as the major issue of contention, to the extent, that the day before the Bills were introduced there was a move in Caucus to add a new paragraph to the Ministerial financial statement that read:

> In view of the present deplorable condition of many thousands of Citizens of Australia through unemployment, and for the purpose of continuing Government undertakings now held up in consequence of the present financial position, and for the purpose of stimulating government activities to improve the economic position generally, the Government will arrange with the Commonwealth Bank to issue Credits on deposited Bonds of the States and Commonwealth, for all Government requirements in lieu of loans.[46]

The economic situation was deteriorating and control of the industrial system in line with the platform was critical to Labor's plan of combating the Depression. On this point Scullin left nothing to members' imaginations in the House about the dire plight of Australia, even likening the economic crises to the crises the country experienced during the World War I:

> We are facing a critical period, and emergency measures may be necessary. Some emergency legislation was passed in wartime, and wartime power was used to safeguard the people. I do not suggest that we are passing through a war period, but some aspects of our financial and economic position today are quite as serious as many of those with

---

[46] The amendment was moved by Yates but was ruled out of order by the Chairman. See; *Caucus Minutes*, 13 March 1930.

which we had to deal during the war. We are passing
through a critical time and our watchword is economy. We
must attempt to balance our trade. We ask for increased
powers so that we may prevent this country from being
exploited from within while we are balancing the trade
from without.[47]

In summing up his case for the adoption of the proposals Scullin
again turned his attention towards the undemocratic nature of the
system for amending the Constitution and made one last plea:

Those who say that the referendum provided for in the
Constitution is democratic mis-state the position ... It is
possible to get a four to one majority vote in favour of an
alteration which yet cannot be carried because it is not
endorsed by a majority of the States. Is that democratic?
... Since 1926 the Commonwealth has enjoyed a new
status; Australia is a nation, and subject to no external
restrictions; and the ties that bind the Empire are mainly
ties of kinship ... [Therefore] we propose to go to the
people, the creators of parliament and the makers of the
Constitution, to ask them to strike off the fetters that bind
the National Parliament.[48]

Whilst Labor was taking the fight up in the Parliament on behalf of
a myriad of Australians who had been devastated by the effects of
the Depression nothing could stop the growing army of people who
were unemployed, destitute and hungry. The plight of this band of
Australians was taken up at rallies and demonstrations where huge
crowds were addressed by people demanding answers and placing
the battlers plight on the public record. One of these rallies was
described in *Labor Call*:

---

[47] *C.P.D.*, Vol. 123, 14 March 1930, p.185.
[48] ibid., p.187.

> In a stirring address, Mr Albert Butler (Flemington, ALP) said there were no signs of any financial stringency or shortage of anything in Melbourne ... Selfishness and the lust for pleasure could be seen in the fashionable streets of Melbourne, while hunger, want, misery and destitution stalked through the land Men, women and also little children, were being herded together in railway carriages and parks at night; the appalling conditions prevailing were a disgrace to civilisation and degrading to human beings.[49]

On 2 April 1930, Scullin called a special meeting of Caucus and explained that Cabinet had given consideration to the worsening unemployment situation, and recommended that the Party introduce another referenda Bill to provide for Trade and Commerce.[50] Caucus duly approved the new measure and on 4 April 1930 the Constitution Alteration (Trade and Commerce) Bill was introduced in the Parliament by Scullin:

> The object of this Bill is that an extra question may be submitted to the electors by referendum. As a matter of fact it was the original intention of the government to submit three questions but Ministers were reluctant to submit more than two, fearing that any other course would confuse the minds of the electors ... The limitations of the Constitution in respect of Trade and Commerce have been grave stumbling blocks to the operation of the National Parliament since federation.[51]

Scullin then outlined the limitations that Labor faced in effectively legislating in the area of trade and commerce in line with the platform and what it hoped to achieve by pursuing the legislation:

---

[49] *Labor Call*, Melbourne, 24 April 1930.
[50] *Caucus Minutes*, 2 April 1930.
[51] *C.P.D.*, Vol. 123, 4 April 1930, p.897.

The trade and commerce limitations upon the Commonwealth are very grave. They are illogical, because who can define what is interstate and what is intrastate commerce; who can determine when commerce ceases to flow across the borders of any state and begins to be interstate, ceasing to be intrastate? ... To a large extent these restrictions of an artificial character on trade and commerce, one of the most important phases of life, make our Constitution ridiculous; as defined, our power is exceedingly narrow ... While I do not suggest that we should take over the complete fixation of prices from beginning to end under the trade and commerce power ... it has occurred that advantage has been taken of our protective duties to exploit the community. We should have the power to stop that kind of thing by regulation or control ... We desire to substitute government of the people by Parliament. If there is to be price fixing it should be done, not by private combines, but by the representatives of the people..[52]

On 10 April 1930 the three referenda Bills passed their third reading in the House on party lines. Labor had forced the political pace and was no longer content to sit back and accept the worsening economic plight of the country as a *fait accompli* or to accept the dictates of Gibson from the Commonwealth Bank on how Labor should fight the Depression. The passage of the referenda proposals through the House provided a clear indication that although Labor was faced with insurmountable obstacles, it still pursued key planks in the platform in the belief that enacting these planks would alleviate the worsening depression. The referenda Bills passed through the House on party lines and were then introduced to the Senate. The passage of the referenda Bills

---

[52] ibid., pp.898-9.

through the Senate also corresponded with Labor's 12th Commonwealth Conference held in Canberra where delegates met to debate the platform and discuss the Government's legislative program in light of the worsening economic climate that was enveloping the country. On 26 May 1930, the day before the Bills were debated in the Senate, the issue of the referenda Bills were discussed by Conference delegates with Drakeford moving:

> That this conference approves of the referenda proposals of the Federal government as being a definite and strong endeavor on the part of the Federal Government to put into operation one of the chief planks of the platform.[53]

Scullin's administration had been in power six months and although fighting to keep its head above water, it had at last faced the Depression head on and was actively pursuing Labor policy as prescribed in the platform in an effort to combat rising unemployment, homelessness and a raft of other social and economic issues that confronted Australia.

Scullin was determined to ensure that Conference unanimously supported the proposals, especially given the fact that they had been passed in the House and were being debated in the Senate. Scullin told delegates that:

> Now they [Labor] were in the responsible position of being a Government and able to take a referendum, they ought to be in a position to know exactly what was in the mind of every Labor party in the Commonwealth. They had a clear and definite platform, that declared for unlimited legislative powers to the Commonwealth Parliament and such delegated powers to the States as the Federal Parliament may from time to time determine. They were

---

[53] Australian Labor Party, <u>Official Report of Proceedings of the 12th Commonwealth Conference</u>, Canberra, 26 May 1930, p.35.

elected with the platform before them, and they felt that there were powers they ought to have at once; principally industrial powers and powers to regulate trade and commerce, because with the control of labour conditions there should be, side by side with that, power to regulate the prices of commodities.[54]

Scullin was concerned that State executives would not back the proposals and that Conference may alter the platform with respect to the goals of pursuing change via referenda. In fact, Scullin like Hughes twenty years earlier had to contend with State Labor executives who were fearful of losing their power. However, despite some opposition from State executives Scullin urged delegates to convince their respective executive branches to 'pledge' support for the proposals whilst they were in the federal Parliament stating:

He was elected on the platform but the conference could alter it. He did not want to be put in the position of saying that it could be modified. He asked delegates to take the position they, as a Government, would be in if they went forth and were not getting the support of men who counted in the states. It was all very well for them to have the parliamentary Labor Party, but if their State executives were not with them, where would they be? If conference was prepared to say now: "We believe in the solidarity of Labor. Go for a measure of the platform", that would not be breaking the platform. If they said: "Go for the whole platform we stand for" he would be delighted, because he had never believed in anything else.[55]

Scullin's appeal to delegates about the need for solidarity to pursue the referenda proposals in line with the platform was not well

---

[54] ibid., p.34.
[55] ibid., p.35.

received by some delegates who raised serious concerns about the impact of referendum proposal number one. One of the most vocal critics of proposal number one was Western Australian delegate Burgess who stated that:

> Speaking as a delegate credentialed by the district council of Fremantle … [he had a] free hand on most agenda items, but on the present question he had most definite and emphatic instructions to oppose it in all its phases … although they might not be able to block the passage of these measures, he was quite satisfied that there would be intense opposition to any extension of Federal political powers.[56]

Similarly, Curtin expressed his concerns about the breadth of proposal number one stating that:

> This question of altering the constitution had behind it a history of defeat, and it had had many complications … At present the people were the masters of the constitution, but with the passage of No.1 it only meant a change of government of the capitalistic order to show its boomerang effect … The Constitution should be amended and the people should be consulted in respect thereto and there should be certain rights reserved for all time to the people and no variation of the constitution except by reference to the people.[57]

At the conclusion of debate on the original motion Calwell moved:

> The motion be taken seriatim in the order of the three subjects involved, namely: (1) Full powers to the Commonwealth; (2) industrial powers; and, (3) relating to trade and commerce powers.[58]

---

[56] ibid., p.38.
[57] ibid., p.37.

The Chairman then read the original motion from Drakeford in conjunction with the three proposals: proposals two and three were carried unanimously, however proposal one was only carried by 22 votes to 13.[59] The Conference debate over the referenda proposals was lively, however Conference ratified Scullin's proposals by twenty-two votes to thirteen with the concerns raised by delegates about the proposals only providing a portent of what Labor could expect during a referenda campaign, if it could get the measures through the Senate. Scullin had secured a victory, however the opposition to the proposals by his own colleagues together with debate about the legality of the proposed Bills had placed him under pressure to re-consider the double dissolution option.

Conference may have endorsed Scullin's call to arms, however his appeal was met with stiff resistance in the Senate and on 28 May 1930 the Opposition in that chamber rejected all three proposals by twenty-two votes to seven on each Bill.[60] The Bills were now potential triggers for a double dissolution which Scullin could place before the Australian people, however on 29 May Scullin informed Caucus that:

> Owing to the difference of opinion of the Crown Law Officers, & the Legal opinion which the Government sought from Sir Harrison Moore & Mr Harbinger, not to take the referendum at present.[61]

The referenda proposals that had been endorsed by Cabinet and by Federal Conference and vigorously defended in the Parliament were effectively dropped by Scullin and any potential double

---

[58] Mr Mooney seconded the motion, see: <u>ibid.</u>, p.48.

[59] see: <u>ibid.</u>, p.48

[60] No opposition Senator voted for the Bills despite the fact that Hughes, Thompson, Corser and Stewart had done so in the House. see; *C.P.D.*, Vol 124, 28 May 1930, pp.2190-1.

[61] *Caucus Minutes*, 29 May 1930.

dissolution trigger as envisaged by members like Anstey was now voided. Scullin had forgone an opportunity to pursue and enact key planks in the platform and make an impact on the Depression by forging ahead with the proposals, instead he chose to believe that Labor could provide a viable policy mix to combat the rising unemployment, destitution and financial woes that were crippling the country. Unfortunately for Scullin and the wider labour movement, history would show otherwise and according to Barrett:

> Labor's basic problem was to decide whether it should challenge the Senate and go to the country on a double dissolution. The party made several decisions to challenge the Senate, but acted on none of them; thus it solved the problem by delay and drift.[62]

Similarly Crisp noted that the referenda Bills:

> … were victims first of the Senate and secondly of the strains and preoccupations of the deepening economic blizzard.[63]

Labor had effectively foregone a vital opportunity to change the political landscape in its favour by placing the Government in a position where it could have controlled both Houses and placed the referenda proposals before the people to provide Labor with the necessary power to combat the Depression by enacting a range of measures including key platform policy planks. However, despite the backdown on the referenda Labor still attempted to pursue planks in the platform notwithstanding the Opposition's stance of killing them off in the Senate.

Wheat and Hops Marketing

---

[62] Barrett, R.H., <u>Promises and Performances in Australian Politics 1928 – 1963</u>. Publications Centre, University of British Columbia, Canada, 1963, p.49.
[63] Crisp, L.F., (1977) <u>op cit</u>., p.46.

In the remainder of the second session Labor introduced legislation to strengthen and enact key planks in the platform, including the introduction of a proposal to establish a Hops and Wheat Marketing Board in line with sub plank 10 of the Platform under the heading 'National Work' that called on Labor to establish 'Australian wide co-operative pools for the marketing and financing of farm products'; the introduction of legislation to establish a Central Reserve Bank in line with plank 1 of the Finance and Taxation Reform section of the platform, and the introduction of Conciliation and Arbitration legislation to strengthen Labor's commitment to the Industrial Reform section of the platform.

On 4 March 1930 Scullin made a famous public broadcast to all Australians when he officially launched a campaign for farmers to 'grow more wheat' to combat the Depression by increasing national exports, in which he told Australians:

> Increase our production of exportable goods. These are necessarily primary products, and the industry which can most readily respond to proposals for increasing production is the wheat growing industry. We must grow more wheat, and we must export more wheat.[64]

Labor positioned itself to assist farmers, especially wheat growers and hops growers proposing two pieces of legislation to enact sub plank 10 of the platform with the introduction of the Wheat Marketing Bill and the Hops Marketing Bill. On 3 April 1930 Caucus approved the Wheat Marketing Bill to be introduced in the House,[65] and the following day, Parker Maloney, Minister for Markets and Transport outlined the Bill to the House:

---

[64] *Argus*, 5 March 1930.
[65] *Caucus Minutes*, 3 April 1930.

> This Bill contains the proposals of the Government for the stabilisation of the wheat industry ... The Government's policy is to stimulate and encourage our primary and secondary industries ... The wheat growing industry is of outstanding importance to the financial stability of the Commonwealth ... The object of the Bill is to regulate the export and interstate trade in wheat and flour through a board, to be known as the Australian Wheat Board, controlled by wheat producers in order to give effect to the government policy for an Australian compulsory wheat pool. The government will guarantee to the growers payment of 4s. a bushel for f.a.q wheat delivered at country railway stations, plus 8d. a bushel for rail freight and other expenses.[66]

Moloney outlined the broad thrust of the Bill, that was expected to bring some relief for farmers as well as improve Australia's export position, and he hoped to receive bipartisan support for its passage:

> I invite the cooperation of all parties in the passage of this Bill, which is designed to assist a large section of our primary producers to whom we are appealing to help Australia out of the economic difficulties which at present surround her.[67]

On 5 June the Bill passed its second reading in the House and appeared to be on track of passing through the Senate where it was supported by a number of Opposition Senators, however it was not until two Country Party members from Western Australia, who initially supported the Bill, voted against it that the measure was resigned to the political scrap heap.[68] Despite the setback Labor

---

[66] *C.P.D.*, Vol. 123, 8 April 1930, pp.916-7.
[67] ibid., pp.924-5.
[68] E. B Johnsonn and W. Carroll, wanted the Second reading debate adjourned

continued to pursue wheat legislation through the Parliament in line with sub-plank 10 of the platform and introduced the Wheat Advances Bill in December 1930. The Bill was substantially modified by the Senate and according to Sawyer:

> ... the Act was a dead letter because the Commonwealth and other Banks refused to co-operate – partly because of financial stringency, but still more because of doubts about the constitutional validity of the Act.[69]

Labor's hopes of enacting sub plank 10 of the platform under the heading 'National Work' had again been dealt a savage blow in the Senate and although it had become common place for the Senate to practically maul every piece of legislation introduced into the chamber, especially legislation attempting to enact Labor platform planks, Labor continued to address Australia's economic and social plight by pursuing the platform.[70]

<u>Central Reserve Bank</u>

The Government now turned its attention towards enacting a key platform plank that was guaranteed to be slaughtered in the Senate, but it fought on regardless. On 1 May 1930 Labor introduced the Central Reserve Bank Bill into the House. The establishment of a Central Reserve Bank was a key plank in the platform with plank 1 of the Finance and Taxation Reform section stating:

---

but the Government refused and the Country Party made this a grievance, in the resulting division the Bill was defeated. See; *C.P.D.*, Vol. 125, 4 July 1930, p.3716.

[69] Sawer, <u>op cit</u>., p.18.

[70] In March 1931 Labor introduced another Wheat Bill that was systematically dismantled clause by clause in the Senate by Archdale Parkhill See; *C.P.D.*, Vol.131, pp.3919, 4770 and 5079. Labor again replaced it with the Wheat Bounty Bill that was finally passed on 30 October 1931.

> The Commonwealth Bank to be developed on the lines of a Central Reserve Bank, while retaining its ordinary and Savings-Bank functions. Its operations to be extended to give greater assistance to the primary and other industries of the country. The Commonwealth Bank to remain, in the matter of policy, free from association or agreement with the private banks.[71]

The Bill moved to separate core central banking functions from the existing Commonwealth Bank and establish and develop them in a new financial institution to be known as the Central Reserve Bank. Theodore introduced the Bill into the House stating:

> The Bill is a proposal for the establishment of an important new financial institution, which it is intended shall operate for the maintenance of the stability and security of Australia's monetary and credit system ... There is a generally held opinion among economists, bankers and financiers generally that our existing banking and financial system has proved defective and that that has been partly responsible for the difficulties which Australia has encountered in the last year or two. The lack of means for the mobilisation of our credit resources has been a serious defect in our monetary system within recent months ... A central bank can aid greatly in tiding a country over a period of financial stringency and credit difficulties by concentrating the reserves of all the banks operating in the country, and enabling the best use to be made of them.[72]

The proposed Bill was a major initiative in line with the platform that sought to reshape the Australian financial landscape. The Bill

---

[71] Australian Labor Party, <u>Official Report of Proceedings of the 12th Commonwealth Conference</u>, Canberra, 26 May 1930, p.4.
[72] *C.P.D.*, Vol. 123, 1 May 1930, p.1334.

proposed that the bank be controlled by a board of nine directors to be appointed by the government of the day; that it would control the note issue of the Commonwealth; that it should have the power to requisition gold and pay for it with notes; that it also have the power to make unsecured loans to the government as well as conduct the financial business of the government. A new Central Reserve Bank would also enable the Commonwealth Bank to compete in the market place with private institutions for ordinary banking business. According to Theodore:

> The Commonwealth Bank was intended to be a trading institution and to operate freely in competition with the private trading banks ... It was only later in its career that an attempt was made to enable it to assume central banking functions. Originally it had not even control of the note issue. Subsequently it was given that control, and an attempt was made to enable it to develop into a central reserve bank; but it has not succeeded in fulfilling the functions of such an institution, and cannot be regarded as a central reserve bank.[73]

The Government had experienced problems in dealing with the Commonwealth Bank and most notably its Chairman Sir Robert Gibson in formulating its policies with respect to combating the dire effects of the Depression, and it was these difficulties, with respect to banking practice and credit expansion, that the Federal Conference debated the Report of the Unemployment Committee. The Unemployment Committee's Report to delegates on 29 May highlighted the difficulties the Government had experienced in implementing its policy agenda to combat unemployment and laid the blame with the banking sector stating:

> In Australia preventable unemployment has been

---

[73] <u>ibid</u>.

aggravated by the restriction of credit due to present banking practice. This has operated to prevent potential employers, ie., manufacturers, agriculturalists, local governing bodies and the like, being able, in the case of the first class, to extend their factories in order to supply the home market which recent tariff policy has secured to them ... Faced today with widespread and increasing unemployment, it is undoubted that the primary duty of Australian Governments, Federal and State, is the provision of adequate food clothing and shelter ... The immediate problem as it presents itself to your committee is twofold in character:

1.   Subsistence relief and work and;
2.   Scientific treatment towards prevention and elimination.

In regard to either or both of the foregoing, the restoration and freeing of credit is an indispensable condition. The Commonwealth Government by reason of the fact that banking is within its legislative jurisdiction, must release the necessary credit.[74]

The Report also highlighted the importance of public works programs and requested the Government to find £20,000,000 and allocate this money to the States to finance public work programs. The Committee echoed the sentiments of all Labor supporters with respect to the provision of expanded public works initiatives and although the rhetoric could not be faulted, the Committee failed to provide the Government with a plausible way of actually obtaining the money. In its conclusion the Committee recommended that:

The general problem [of abnormal unemployment] is

---

[74] Australian Labor Party, <u>Official Report of Proceedings of the 12</u>th <u>Commonwealth Conference</u>, Canberra, 29 May 1930, pp.66-7.

inherent in the existing economic system, the remedy for which is the realisation of the policy set out in the objects and platform of the Australian Labor Party.[75]

Conference delegates unanimously endorsed the report and also endorsed Labor to pursue plank 1 of the new Progressive Reform section of its platform under Banking which called for the 'Institution of a Commonwealth Reserve Bank.'[76] The Bill progressed through the House and according to Schedvin:

> ... was accorded a quiet and reasonably sympathetic reception.'[77]

The trading banks were not unduly critical of the legislation and their main complaint was that they had not been consulted on the details of the Bill.[78] The Bill passed the second and third readings in the House without division and apart from a few members of Labor's left wing, who considered the Bill too financially orthodox for their liking, such as Yates who described it as leaving him 'stone cold', it had a relatively unaffected passage through the House. However, it was not until the Bill reached the Senate that the Opposition set about destroying it and according to Schedvin:

> There was an extraordinary change in the opposition's attitude. They now saw no merit in it [the Bill] whatsoever. As the debate progressed, purely banking considerations were pushed aside and the main issues were political.[79]

The major political consideration raised by the Opposition focused

---

[75] Australian Labor Party, <u>Official Report of Proceedings of the 12th Commonwealth Conference</u>, Canberra, 29 May 1930, p.67.
[76] see; <u>ibid</u>, 26 May 1930, p.4.
[77] Schedvin, <u>op cit.</u>, p.173.
[78] Davidson to Shann, 31 March 1930, BNSWA as cited in <u>ibid</u>.
[79] <u>ibid</u>.

upon causing maximum political damage to Theodore who was, at the time, the centre of a Queensland Nationalist Government's Royal Commission into his involvement in the sale of silver and lead mines at Mungana when he was Premier of the State.[80] On 4 July the Royal Commission released its findings and found that Theodore was guilty of the 'grossest impropriety'.[81] Theodore protested his innocence and resigned as Treasurer so that he could return to Queensland to fight the charges. The loss to Labor of Theodore was immense, for as well as attempting to steer the Central Reserve Bank Bill through the Parliament, Theodore was heavily involved in finalising the federal budget and had been notified by Scullin that he (Theodore) would lead Labor and be caretaker Prime Minister whilst Scullin attended an Imperial Conference in London (Scullin would be absent for at least 3 months).

On 10 July, the Opposition in the Senate moved to capitalise on Labor's predicament and passed a motion to refer the Central Reserve Bank Bill to a select committee comprised entirely of Opposition Senators. The Bill then sat in Committee until December when the Committee handed down a report finding that although it was in favour of the principle of a central reserve bank, the economic circumstances were such that it was inappropriate to introduce such legislation in the middle of a Depression. The report also noted that the proposed Bank would be subject to political pressure due to the appointment of Board members by the Government. After the report was handed down the Bill was carried over to be read in a further six months' time. Unfortunately for Labor, the economic conditions that beset the country were worsening on a daily basis and although the

---

[80] For a detailed analysis of the Mungana Royal Commission and its findings see; Kennedy. K., The Mungana Affair. University of Queensland Press, Brisbane, 1978.

[81] ibid., p.75.

Government attempted to reintroduce the Central Reserve Bank Bill in every session the Bill was eventually abandoned when the Government was defeated in 1931. Labor had again hit the proverbial brick wall in the Senate with the Opposition using its numbers in the chamber to dismantle legislation and keep Labor under a constant state of siege.

Scullin's decision not to pursue a double dissolution arguably impacted on Labor's ability to successfully pursue the platform, for if Labor controlled the Senate then important initiatives like Wheat and Hops Marketing and the establishment of a Central Reserve Bank, both important planks in the platform, could have become a reality. However, this was not to be and although important measures were being summarily executed in the Senate, Labor continued to pursue the platform in the hope that its legislation would not attract a bullet.

Conciliation and Arbitration

On 30 May 1930, the day after Scullin had retreated on the double dissolution threat, the Attorney General, Brennan introduced the Conciliation and Arbitration Bill into the House to strengthen the existing industrial relations planks in the platform:

> Peace, in industry, remains an ideal devoutly to be wished for. The Government has a mission to proceed unfalteringly along the rugged path that leads to this result; and an emphatic mandate to employ for that purpose the processes of conciliation and arbitration.[82]

Industrial peace may have been the wish, however the Government was pursuing a complete overhaul of existing industrial legislation. The three main principles contained in the

---

[82] *C.P.D.*, Vol. 124, 30 May 1930, p.2362.

Bill that the Government were pursuing were:

1. substantially modifying the penalties against strikes and lockouts;

2. providing Commissioners with award making and judicial powers; and

3. the creation of Conciliation Committees with the power of majority decision.

Brennan then cited Hansard excerpts in which the leadership of the Opposition (primarily Latham and Bruce) had publicly declared their support for the system of conciliation and arbitration[83] and he declared:

> These quotations, which need not be elaborated, bring out in strong relief the fact that honourable members opposite, as well as honourable members on this side of the House, are deeply pledged, by their votes and through their leaders, to this policy of industrial conciliation and arbitration.[84]

Brennan may have been somewhat optimistic in believing that the Opposition would support the proposal based on comments that were made in the late 1920s, but there was no denying the position that Federal Conference had taken on the issue. On 29 May, the day before the Bill was introduced in the House, Conference delegates adopted the recommendations contained in the Report of the Committee on Industrial Relations: stating

> The Committee had perused the proposed Bill and recommended to delegates:

---

[83] ibid., pp.2362-3.
[84] ibid., p.2363.

1. That the Conciliation and Arbitration Act should be amended as early as possible; In order to give effect to the policy of the Government as outlined in the Prime Minister's policy speech:

2. The Arbitration Act to be revised to provide for a system of sound, business like arbitration, free from the entangling legalisms of the law court ... to be to ensure equitable, expeditious and less costly methods of dealing with industrial matters.

3. The alterations of the Act should provide forthwith for the judges being confined to purely legal functions, and that the conciliation and arbitral functions of the court be exercised by the industrial commissioners.

4. That the improvements foreshadowed in the proposed Act are approved of as an instalment of arbitration reform in the direction of conciliation, but the Government be requested as soon as possible, ~~or when further powers are obtained~~, to *immediately* bring the Act into line with the desires of the industrial movement;[85]

5. That the decisions of conference on the recommendations contained herein be immediately conveyed to the government.[86]

The Committee recommended the adoption of the Report, however Drakeford informed the Conference that:

This Act which Mr Brennan proposed to put through did not express by any means what the ACTU desired ... for example, the creation of a Bureau of Statistics, which would

---

[85] The amendments to section 3 were moved by Duggan and Jude. See; <u>Australian Labor Party Official Report of proceedings of the 12th Commonwealth Conference</u>. Canberra, 29 May 1930, p.70.

[86] The Report Committee comprised of A.S Drakeford; W.J. Riordan; T.M. Jude; J. Hooke; H. Kneebone and P.J. Mooney, <u>Australian Labor Party Official Report of proceedings of the 12th Commonwealth Conference</u>. Canberra, 29 May 1930, p.70.

gather information as to the effect of wages awards and the area and extent of unemployment ... The question of preference to unionists was not being insisted upon. [also] The position had been reached where the various judges of the Court had said that they proposed to deal with the basic wage, and in all probability reduce it ... Referring to section 2, when it [the Act] was altered in the way the industrialists desired, it might be essential to have only one judge with High Court powers. There was no idea of dictation at all.[87]

Conference delegates were aware of the shortcomings of the proposed legislation but approved of the government proceeding with the Bill. With the support of Conference Brennan reiterated the Government's commitment to industrial arbitration stating:

This Government bears in mind the pledges which it gave to the people and the mandate that it received at their hands in regard to the maintenance of basic standards. That is the substance of the solemn compact on this subject between the Parliament and the electors. Faced with unprecedented financial obligations and responsibilities, the Government stands firm to its accepted promise and pledge on this vital matter, recognising, as it does, that the undermining of basic standards must be reflected in increased destitution, reduced purchasing power, inroads upon the primary necessities of the working class in the community, with the consequent and dangerous impairment of national security and solvency.[88]

Brennan elucidated the significance of the Bill and made a plea to

---

[87] Australian Labor Party Official Report of proceedings of the 12th Commonwealth Conference. Canberra, 29 May 1930, p.70.
[88] *C.P.D.*, Vol. 124, 30 May 1930, p.2365.

the leadership of the Opposition that:

> On the main principles I am entitled to hope that the
> Leader of the Opposition (Mr Latham) will be in agreement
> with the Government; on matters of detail we can afford to
> differ.[89]

Unfortunately for Brennan and for Labor his plea went unheeded
and after a relatively uneventful passage through the House and
the Senate, where it passed the second reading in both chambers,
the Opposition set about dismantling the legislation in the
Committee stages of debate on the Bill. The Bill then returned to
the House with thirty amendments that completely altered its form
and scope. On 7 August Scullin decided to negotiate the proposed
amendments via managers with representatives from all sides and
both Houses being present, with the resulting meeting literally
lasting all night and extending into the early hours of the next day.[90]
The compromised Bill that had been agreed to by the leadership of
both Parties limped back into the House where Latham extolled:

> In some respects it is a new Bill; but I am not trying to score
> a party advantage. Neither side has secured everything it
> wanted.[91]

Latham was correct, neither side secured everything that it wanted,
however Labor had received an overwhelming electoral mandate
to restructure the industrial relations system in line with its stated
platform policy goals. On this occasion the Senate did not kill the
Bill. It ensured that the revised Bill was a pale imitation of what it
should have been. The impact of the amendments were not lost on

---

[89] ibid., p.2363.
[90] Beasley, McTiernan, Chifley, Daley and Barnes represented Labor and
Pearce, McLachlan and Johnston for the opposition. See; *C.P.D.*, Vol. 124, 8
August 1930, pp.5664-5.
[91] ibid, p.5665.

Labor members who spoke to the new Bill, with Martens providing a moderate response in comparison with others stating:

> I regret that this Government has not been able to give effect to the arbitration legislation that originally introduced; but I am prepared to support the compromise.[92]

Martens then qualified his position further by stating:

> I have a keen appreciation of the slaughter that will take place among the workers if this House adjourns without amending the Arbitration Act ... This compromise is far from what the great mass of the workers want; but still it is the best that we can do for them, and, if accepted, it will to some extent alleviate the oppressive conditions under which they are working.[93]

Lazzarini was not as restrained as Martens and launched a stinging attack on Latham and the amendments that had decimated the Bill stating:

> There is an old saying that the victor can afford to be generous ... but it is a little late in the day for him [Latham] to talk about sweet reasonableness and compromise, for the wreckage of industry is lying all around us ... When the Attorney General introduced this Bill, he said that it did not by any means give effect to the full objective of the labour movement in regard to industry, but represented the very least that could be accepted.[94]

Lazzarini was incensed that the Bill had effectively been destroyed by the Opposition in the Senate, even making reference to the

---

[92] ibid., p.5673.
[93] ibid.
[94] ibid., p.5671.

need for Labor to pursue a double dissolution to ensure that Labor policy could be enacted:

> The Senate has torn the Bill to shreds ... The Senate is, metaphorically speaking, putting its fingers to its nose, and treating this House with contempt. While the Labor Party was returned to power with an overwhelming majority, and a mandate from the people to improve our industrial machinery, none of the members of another place [the Senate] faced the electors. We have a superior army, but have thrown away our guns, and hoisted the white flag of surrender. In my opinion, the Government should close this abortive session, and call honourable members together as early as possible in October, and send the members of another place [the Senate] to their masters.[95]

Lazzarini's comments, although emotionally based, held some political weight for the Government had had the opportunity to go to the people and attempt to clean out the Senate and in light of the destruction of the Government's most important legislative policy prescriptions it certainly was a valid option. At the close of the second parliamentary session Labor's legislative program was a shambles and according to Robertson:

> By this time its [the Government's] program should have been in full swing. Instead, its troubles were mounting; unemployment had risen to over 20% and wage rates were on a downward spiral. [96]

In his biography on Scullin, Robertson also discussed Labor's legislative program:

---

[95] ibid.
[96] Robertson, op cit., p.185.

> The parliamentary period had been something of a disappointment to him [Scullin]. Much had been attempted, not a great deal achieved. Twelve Bills, most of them important, had not become law. There was no sign of a double dissolution. The Government had made some attempts to balance its budget, it had raised tariffs, and had made a relief grant of £1 million; but unemployment was increasing. In Parliament, in public statements, and in addresses to unionists, Scullin had argued that his government had done all it could.[97]

The government had attempted to pursue and enact the platform but with very limited success, due in large part to the fact that Labor did not control the very basic levers of government. In fact, Labor's problems were further exacerbated when the government effectively handed control of the Government's policy agenda to Sir Robert Gibson the head of the Commonwealth Bank, and Sir Otto Niemeyer from the Bank of England.

---

[97] ibid., p.258.

4 THE FRACTURING OF CAUCUS AND THE DEMISE OF THE SCULLIN GOVERNMENT

Gibson and Niemeyer would literally prescribe federal Labor policy for the remainder of the Government's term in office and enacting Labor's platform was not a part of either man's policy agenda for combating the Depression. On 7 April 1930 the Deputy Governor of the Bank of England, Sir Ernest Harvey, cabled Gibson with concerns about Australia's ability to pay its loan obligations stating:

> We here are genuinely anxious to try and find suitable means whereby Australia may be helped to overcome present difficulties. Full consideration is being given to the matter but at present are seriously handicapped by lack of full authoritative information. It is important we should have before us most complete particulars available both of immediate specific proposals and of any general plan for righting situation over a period of time.[98]

The Bank of England had become increasingly concerned about the Government potentially defaulting on its loan commitments as well as its policy prescriptions in a number of areas, most notably Australia's apparent failure to conform to the rules of the gold standard as well as the fact that the government had not contracted

---

[98] Schedvin, op cit., p.133.

the note issue in proportion to its gold reserves. Harvey followed his initial cable with a stronger version on 7 May and it was at this point that Gibson and Harvey in effect plotted a peaceful coup and resolved to send out a representative of the Bank, in this case Sir Otto Niemeyer,[99] to analyse government policy and provide a program to combat the concerns of the Bank of England.

Scullin had the opportunity to deny Gibson's and Harvey's request, however within a week of the request going to the government Scullin had agreed on the proviso of 'full disclosure' of Niemeyer's findings. Also, in respect of Gibson, Scullin incurred the ire of Caucus when he re-appointed him to his position as Chairman of the Commonwealth Bank without informing Caucus of his intention to do so with the *Sydney Morning Herald* reporting:

> Scullin had promised to allow Caucus to discuss the appointment before any decision was made but he had not honoured that promise.[100]

Scullin's announcement that he had re-appointed Gibson was not released until 15 August,[101] the date is significant because Parliament was in recess and the Caucus had held its last meeting a week earlier on 6 August.[102] Gibson had been an arch critic of the Scullin administration and its policy platform since its election and he did everything in his power to make life difficult for Labor. Scullin's action incensed Caucus members and on 30 October when Caucus met, Eldridge gave notice that at the first meeting

---

[99] Sir Otto Niemeyer was experienced in the areas of banking and finance. He had joined the British Treasury in 1906 and had been the Controller of Finance for 6 years. He transferred to the Bank of England in 1927 specialising in central banking procedures and problems of national finance.

[100] *Sydney Morning Herald*, 9 September 1930.

[101] Scullin had informed Gibson of his re-appointment on 11 August. The appointment was then reported in the press, see; the *Sydney Morning Herald* and the *Argus*, 15 August 1930.

[102] Federal Cabinet confirmed the appointment on 4 and 8 August 1930.

which the Prime Minister be present that he would move a motion of disapproval of the reappointment of Gibson.[103]

On 14 July Niemeyer arrived in Australia and set about studying the documents being prepared by Treasury for the forthcoming federal budget as well as speaking with political and business leaders and public servants about the state of the Australian economy. If there was any doubt that Niemeyer was not in Australia with the intent of dictating government policy on behalf of the Bank of England it was expelled in an exchange he had with the Speaker of the House Makin who had asked Niemeyer if he [Niemeyer] was having a satisfactory visit, to which Niemeyer pompously replied, 'That depends on whether you do as you are told.'[104]

On 18 August Niemeyer outlined his report to Federal and State Ministers at a Premiers' Conference stating:

> Australian credit is at a low ebb ... lower than that of any of the other dominions ... Australia is off budget equilibrium, off exchange equilibrium, and faced by considerable unfunded and maturing debts, both internally and externally; in addition to which she has on her hands a very large program of loan works, for which no financial provision has been made. The only minor alleviation of a gloomy picture is that, apart from the £36,000,000 of unfunded debt, Australia, by a great piece of luck, has no external maturities in 1930 and 1931. That means, in effect, that she has a maximum period of two years in which to put her house straight ... It is certain that the rate

---

[103] See; Eldridge's notice in the *Argus* 29 October 1930.
[104] Lonie, J., Good Labor Men: The Hill Government in South Australia, 1930-1933, *Labour History* 31, 1976, p.20, note 36.

of increase of output per capita in other countries in recent years is much greater than that of Australia.[105]

Niemeyer's findings became the subject of an extraordinary Cabinet meeting on 20 August held at Scullin's residence in Melbourne. Scullin had been unable to attend the Conference due to the fact that he had developed pleurisy and was in a bad state of health, but he oversaw a four hour meeting the *Sydney Morning Herald* described as:

> ... one of the most vital in the history of the Commonwealth.[106]

Gibson was also present at the meeting asserting that the Government had to reduce its costs as the limit of Bank credit was diminishing. The following day all State Premiers unanimously passed resolutions together with the Federal Government adopting the Niemeyer-Gibson policy package.

The following day all State Premiers unanimously passed five resolutions together with the Federal Government adopting the Niemeyer-Gibson policy package::[107]

> 1. That the several Governments represented at this conference declare their fixed determination to balance their respective budgets for the financial year 1930-1931, and to maintain a similar balanced budget in future years. This budget equilibrium will be maintained on such a basis as is consistent with the repayment or conversion in Australia of Existing

---

[105] *Sydney Morning Herald*, 22 August 1930.

[106] ibid.

[107] The Conference also agreed on three minor resolutions covering the establishment of a standing committee with representatives from all states; the question of duplication of services and thirdly a claim by South Australia for further financial assistance.

internal maturing debt in the next few years. Further, if during any financial year there are indications of a failure of revenue to meet expenditure, immediate further steps will be taken during the year to ensure that the budgets shall balance.

2. That the Loan Council raise no further loans overseas until after existing overseas short term indebtedness has been completely dealt with. This decision to apply to overseas borrowing by large public authorities, in controlling the operations of which the State Treasurer concerned will act in agreement with his colleagues on the Loan Council.

3. That it is resolved by the several Governments, as regards such public works as it may be possible to finance by loans raised in the internal market, that approval will not be given to the undertaking of any new works which are not reproductive, in the sense of yielding to the treasury concerned within a reasonable period a revenue at least equal to the service of the debt (interest and sinking fund.

4. That in order to secure the regular service of the public debt from revenue, steps will be taken to provide that all interest payments shall be made to a special account in the Commonwealth Bank, to be used solely for the payment of interest.

5. That the Commonwealth and State Treasurers will publish monthly, in Australia and overseas, a brief summary on uniform lines showing their budget revenue and expenditure, the position of their short term debt, and the state of the loan account; such

statements to be drawn up after a uniform model to be agreed upon.[108]

The policy package became known as the 'Melbourne Agreement' and it locked the Federal Government into implementing policies that had strict economies and balanced budgets in direct contradiction to Labor's platform. The wider labour movement and the Labor radicals were scathing in their attacks on the agreement with the *Australian Worker* bitterly condemning the Conference resolutions:

> We have recently had the ignominious spectacle of the Premiers of the great Australian nation sitting like a class of schoolboys to be lectured by an emissary of British moneylenders, and told how they should govern their own land. It made one hang one's head in shame. Do the Premiers admit they are incompetent? Do they confess to unfitness for their jobs? Then why not resign en masse, and let Sir Otto Niemeyer assume in fact the dictatorship he is virtually exercising now?

> … To put it bluntly, the workers of Australia must eat cheaper food, and wear shabbier clothes, and give up their few pleasures, in order that Britain's wealthiest loafers may add superfluity to superfluity and wallow still more grossly in sybaritic excess.

> Hundreds of thousands of workers are unemployed today. In all directions there is heart rendering distress. Men, women and children are starving. Many have not a decent roof above their heads. Such poverty, such suffering, has not been seen in Australia Before.

---

[108] *The Age*, Melbourne, 22 August 1930.

And all because rapacious hands are reaching across the seas and stripping us bare.[109]

The condemnation by the *Australian Worker* of Niemeyer's economic medicine would be used to great affect by the moderates and radicals in Caucus who found the Melbourne Agreement an anathema to all they stood for. Also, in the wake of Niemeyer's report, the Federal Executive of the Labor Party met to discuss the crisis and unanimously passed a resolution outlining their program for Scullin to adopt, affirming that:

> Faced with conditions unprecedented in the history of Australia and the necessity for the Labor Movement acting in complete unison in protecting the interests of the masses of the people, this Federal Executive of the ALP, acting in accordance with its constitution, declares that … this attack being the result of long and studied preparation, can only be successfully defeated by the united opposition of Labor.

> After a careful analysis of the economic conditions … this Executive emphatically submits that the economic position can be adjusted by Labor statesmanship adhering to the clearly defined principles of the Labor Movement as expressed in its platform, particularly such planks as those dealing with Banking, Insurance and Arbitration.

> We therefore declare as follows: We are convinced that the only solution of the problems confronting Australia lies in giving effect to Labor's Platform and we direct attention particularly to the planks dealing with Banking, Insurance and Arbitration.

> As a necessary corrective to the wage reduction

---

[109] *Australian Worker*, Sydney, 27 August 1930.

propaganda, which is causing increased unemployment, we believe that:

1. There should be immediately instituted a 'Back to Work' campaign

2. Industry should be stimulated by making credits immediately available

3. By the utilisation of the nation's credit the annual interest burden on internal loan commitments should be progressively eliminated by liquidation of such loans as they mature.

4. There should be a reduction of interest on bank credits advanced to industry.

5. In view of our per capita obligations resulting from the war, negotiations between the Governments of Britain and Australia should result in terms being agreed upon more in keeping with conditions applying to the war indebtedness of other British and foreign counties.[110]

The prescriptions of Labor's Federal Executive were ignored by Scullin who on 25 August, a few days after the Premiers' Conference and Federal Executive meeting, sailed to London to attend the Imperial Conference. Scullin held the view that Australia should be represented by its Prime Minister especially in discussions concerning its economic state and financial future. However, according to Robertson:

---

[110] Weller, P., & Lloyd, B., <u>Federal Executive Minutes, 1915-1955 : minutes of the meetings of the Federal Executive of the Australian Labor Party</u>. Melbourne University Press, Australia, 1978, p.147-8; 151-2.

After Scullin's departure, Australian politics entered a crisis.[111]

With Theodore in Queensland fighting for his political life, Scullin placed two Labor 'conservatives' in charge of the party and the country, a decision that would have severe repercussions. Fenton took up the role as acting Prime Minister whilst Scullin's close friend Lyons was given the Treasury. After perusing the budget records of his new portfolio Lyons became convinced that the Government would have to economise even further from that outlined in the Melbourne Agreement and called a special meeting of Cabinet to discuss the issue. Unfortunately for Lyons the subsequent Cabinet meeting, attended by only seven ministers, divided into two groups; the orthodox conservatives siding with Lyons and Fenton urging further reductions in government spending, whilst the economic moderates comprising of Anstey, Daley and Beasley advocated credit expansion and an inflation of the note issue. The split in Cabinet over Niemeyer's plan provided a portent of the major splits and factions that would soon emerge within Labor in response to combating the financial crisis confronting the country especially in the face of Niemeyer's prescription of tighter economies and balanced budgets. An overwhelming majority of Caucus members believed that balanced budgets and spending restraint would not create employment or provide food or shelter for the growing bands of itinerant workers and families that needed help and it was just a matter of time before the issue came to a head.

On 25 October 'Jack' Lang was elected as Premier of New South Wales on a platform in opposition to Niemeyer and the Melbourne Agreement. Two days after Lang's victory Caucus met and carried a motion congratulating Lang. [112] With Scullin out of the country

---

[111] Robertson, op cit., p.271.
[112] The motion by Lazarrinni stated, 'That a letter of congratulations be forwarded to Mr J.T Lang, Leader of the NSW Labor Party, on the

and on the back of Lang's victory in New South Wales the more radical elements in Caucus began to flex their muscles and on 27 October they carried a motion in opposition to Niemeyer's plan:

> That this Caucus disagrees with the Tariff and industrial Policy initiated by Sir Otto Niemeyer in his address published at the conclusion of the Premiers Conference in Melbourne, and affirms that the Tariff, and industrial policy of Australia are domestic matters to be determined by the people of Australia.[113]

Caucus' position was resolute, they wanted Labor to pursue the platform. On 30 October, Theodore, who had returned from Queensland, quickly moved to introduce an expansionary economic policy to combat the Depression in line with the platform and after a heated debate it was carried on the hands by twenty-six votes to fourteen outlining the Government's financial proposals for combating the Depression:

> 1. That the Commonwealth Bank be required to create sufficient credit, as and when required, for the following purposes:
>
>   (a) Finance the requirements of the Commonwealth Government in connection with all services covered by Parliamentary appropriations.
>   (b) Meet that proportion of the internal loans maturing during the financial year which has not been otherwise provided for.

---

magnificent success of the Party at the recent State elections.' *Caucus Minutes*, 27 October 1930.
[113] ibid.

(c)   Provide for financing State and Commonwealth loan works programs up to a limit of £20,000,000.

(d)   Provide financial accommodation through the Commonwealth Bank, trading Bank, State financial institutions and, if necessary, through insurance companies, to be used for productive purposes in primary and secondary industries. The ultimate amount of credit to be issued under this head to be determined by the effect upon the commodity price levels.

2.   The Credit under the various heads be made available at an interest rate not exceeding 5% per annum.

3.   An effective exchange pool be continued to provide Australian Government with first claim on Australian funds in London. The external exchange rates to be fixed at such rates as will give primary producers the full benefit of the exchange premium on their exports to compensate for the diminished market prices.[114]

Caucus's proposals offered hope to the ever growing army of the destitute and poor whose position had appreciably worsened, with the *Sydney Morning Herald* providing a sombre overview of the situation:

> During recent months the growth of begging in Sydney's streets has been a feature of the city's life ... Now a new army is augmenting their ranks ... Lurking in an alley-way, a man pushes his stunted child forward to offer onion pickles, home made toffee:

> 'Has the gentleman a coin ... sick mother ... please sir!'

---

[114] *Caucus Minutes*, 30 October 1930.

> Thin faces dart from doorways-ties, handkerchiefs, face
> cream, shoe laces, posies, fish that waggle fins; unshaven
> chins, unwashed necks, collarless, shirtless, sockless, tense
> faces; 'Buy, buy, buy, give, give, give;' fierce whispers, the
> failure, the dart back to cover, the next prospect; 'ere y'are,
> sir, very cheap, sir;' eager thrusting, tenacious, imploring.
>
> Some offer nothing, some sing, make pretense at playing
> violins, clarinets, anything. Some just stand and look with
> hunger in their eyes. When the sun drops, the still lower
> orders rake the garbage tins – hooking, stirring: 'nothing'
> 'ere, Jack'.[115]

On 6 November acting Prime Minister Fenton read a cable to
Caucus from Scullin:

> ... that supported the minority vote against Theodore's
> plan and opposed the expansion of credit and any threats to
> coerce the banks.[116]

Scullin asserted:

> ... all this talk about creating credit and inflation is most
> damaging to Australia's reputation in London financial
> circles ... [and added that] Government cannot
> deliberately coerce the administration of the Banks.[117]

The question of coercion was directly linked with threats to
repudiate loan commitments on the Government's loans. The
fractures that were appearing in Caucus reached flash point after
Fenton raised the issue of a £27,000,000 internal loan that was due
in December, and duly ignoring the Government's recent

---

[115] *Sydney Morning Herald*, 12 September 1930.
[116] *Caucus Minutes*, 6 November 1930.
[117] McMullin, 1991, op cit., p.166.

endorsement of the Theodore plan, recommended:

> ... that he should be authorised to advise the Loan Council
> to issue the Loan under three options: 6% for two years;
> 5.75% for ten years or 5.5% for twenty years.'[118]

Curtin and Anstey then successfully carried a motion, in opposition
to Fenton's proposal:

> That the Cabinet as a whole meet the Directors of the
> Commonwealth Bank prior to the meeting of the Loan
> Council and require the Directors to meet the loan ... in
> anticipation of the Directors failing to do this, that a Bill be
> at once prepared and presented to Parliament, renewing for
> a period of twelve months the £27,000,000 loans falling
> due between this and the end of December.[119]

The motion proved too much for Lyons who threatened to resign:

> I will not do it ... I will go out of public life first. I will
> cable the Prime Minister and if he wants it done then he
> must get someone else to do it.[120]

Lyons cabled Scullin and informed him of Caucus' decision.
Scullin was unequivocal in his support for Lyons stating:

> I do not approve and will not support a resolution of the
> party, which I agree is repudiation, which is dishonest and
> disastrous.[121]

On 12 November a special Caucus meeting met to resolve the issue
in light of Scullin's stance and unanimously passed a strongly

---

[118] *Caucus Minutes*, 6 November 1930.
[119] ibid., the motion was carried by 22 votes to 16.
[120] McMullin, 1991, op cit., p.166.
[121] ibid.

worded resolution denying that it had planned to repudiate on the payment of government loans stating:

> That this meeting of the Federal Parliamentary Labor Party strongly depreciates, and emphatically denies any suggestion of, or association with, the repudiation of any financial obligation and will faithfully discharge all lawful commitments. Any attempts to construe Labor's financial proposals to the contrary is false.[122]

Caucus had flexed its muscles and retreated, however the fractures within the Party had deepened. Fenton and Lyons were firmly of the view that Niemeyer was correct in his assessment of what Australian economic and financial policy should be and that the party should be enacting the Melbourne Agreement without delay. To Fenton and Lyons, who were economic conservatives, any policy directives towards credit expansion and inflation of the note issue along the lines advocated in the Theodore Plan would be disastrous for the country. The only problem for Fenton and Lyons was that an overwhelming majority of the Caucus did not agree with them and supported either the Theodore or Lang Plans. With Scullin still out of the country and not expected back until the New Year, Labor found itself floundering.

At the conclusion of the third parliamentary session in December 1930 Labor had introduced no policy initiatives based on the platform and during the entire sitting only twenty-three Acts were passed, of which fourteen were either income tax or sales tax amendments.[123] Labor had lost all traction and any thought of pursuing the platform in the political and economic circumstances of the time was now a pipe dream.

---

[122] *Caucus Minutes*, 12 November 1930.
[123] For an overview of the Acts of the sitting see; *C.P.D.*, Vol. 127, 30 October – 18 December 1930.

Fourth Parliamentary Session

On 4 March 1931 the fourth parliamentary session began and within three days of the resumption the Government had already faced a censure motion[124] and was at the polls for a by election for the seat of East Sydney that was won by the Lang Labor candidate, Mr Eddie Ward. In his maiden speech, which co-incidentally was the debate on the censure motion against the government, Ward stated:

> I have been elected on a very definite policy. The electors of East Sydney are dissatisfied with the inaction of the present government, because they consider, as I too consider, that the present Commonwealth Ministers have wasted wonderful opportunities for doing things which the majority at their command has given them ... If Ministers ... had not been content to be merely seat warmers and timeservers, this Parliament would have been back to the country three months after it was elected. They have lost the confidence of the people because they have lacked courage.[125]

Ward was scathing in his assessment of the government, and although Labor had not proceeded with a double dissolution election, his charge that the government 'lacked courage' is slightly disingenuous given the debilitated and parlous economy and the political situation in the Senate. The government was now operating in survival mode, pursuing the platform was no longer a realistic option and on 26 January Scullin recommended to Caucus that Theodore be reinstated as Treasurer, the fallout of this move producing the first major split within the government under his

---

[124] *C.P.D.*, Vol. 128, 6 March 1931, p.10. (The Government also faced another censure motion on 8 May 1931.)
[125] *C.P.D.*, Vol. 128, 12 March 1931, p.251.

leadership.[126]   Scullin's recommendation was carried by twenty-four votes to nineteen and further divided the radicals from the more conservative members in Caucus. A few hours after the Caucus vote Gabb from South Australia resigned stating:

> I have lost faith in your judgement as a leader ... I am sure you have chosen wrongly.[127]

Gabb's resignation would in fact be the first of a number of government members to take this option and three days later on 29 January Fenton and Lyons resigned from Cabinet and relinquished their ministerial portfolios.

The Lang Plan

On 6 February 1931 a special Premiers' Conference assembled in Canberra to discuss establishing a viable economic policy to combat the depression with Scullin informing the assembled Premiers that the reason for the Conference was that:

> ... no one government, could be expected to prepare a plan in which all governments are to share.[128]

When Scullin ended his speech Lang wanted to know what plans the Federal Government had to combat the Depression:

> There is no plan. As I pointed out to the Premiers when I called them together, the idea of holding this conference was to evolve one.[129]

This admission by Scullin handed the tactical advantage to Lang,

---

[126] see; *Caucus Minutes*, 18 February 1931.
[127] *Argus*, 28 January 1931.
[128] Proceedings and Decisions of the Conference of Commonwealth and State Ministers. *Commonwealth Parliamentary Papers*, Vol. II, February 1931, p.87.
[129] ibid., p.7.

who then effectively hijacked the Conference announcing his own plan for combating the depression by the implementation of a three point plan:

1. Australian governments should pay no further interest to British bondholders until Britain had dealt with the Australian debt in terms comparable to those she had obtained for her own debt to the US. [Lang's policy was repudiation writ large.]

2. The reduction to 3% of interest on all Government borrowings in Australia.

3. Immediate steps be taken to abandon the gold standard in favour of a currency based upon the wealth of Australia, to be termed 'the goods standard'.[130]

The *Labor Daily* supported Lang's bold plan and outlined the rationale behind the plan:

Mr Lang does not see why Australian workers should sweat themselves to skeletons in a time of stress created by financial manipulation for the sake of paying more than a fair thing to those who are prepared to bleed this country white financially.

Therefore he suggests that no further interest be paid to British bondholders until Britain is prepared to make more equitable arrangements in regard to Australia's debts, that the interest payable on all Government borrowing in Australia be reduced to 3% and that the precious gold standard – be abolished.[131]

Lang had stunned the Conference with his proposal, however Scullin and Theodore locked the rest of the Premiers behind the

---

[130] *Sydney Morning Herald*, 10 February 1931.
[131] *Labor Daily*, 11 February 1931.

Theodore Plan that relied heavily on the Commonwealth Bank co-operating with the Government by advancing credit to the government to stimulate the economy. The Conference had achieved a result, however it was a result that saw two Labor leaders, Lang and Scullin, committing their respective Labor Governments to different policy agendas to combat the depression.

The 'Lang Plan' as it became known split Labor down the middle and accentuated the split between the New South Wales branch and the Federal executive of the Party. On 18 February Caucus:

> ... approved of the Commonwealth Government continuing negotiations with the (Commonwealth Bank) on the lines laid down by the Prime Minister and Mr Theodore ... [for the implementation of the Theodore Plan].[132]

Caucus also recommended that in the event that they were unsuccessful:

> ... the Government immediately proceed to secure Legislative power to give effect to the Party's Platform on Banking and Currency.[133]

Caucus advocated a double dissolution followed by an assault on the platform, if Labor won the election and controlled the Senate, however Scullin remained adamant that the Theodore plan was the only policy that Labor would pursue in Parliament. A double dissolution, together with pursuing the platform was not considered. Scullin told Caucus that he:

> ... was not going to take dictation from any one section of the movement.[134]

---

[132] *Caucus Minutes*, 18 February 1931.
[133] ibid.

Scullin then indicated that he would move to expel any member of the Government who supported the Lang plan, to which Eldridge replied:

> ... here's one who's going to do it, put me out now.[135]

Eldridge remained in the Party until the election of Ward and on 12 March Scullin ruled in Caucus that:

> ... any member elected on any other policy [other than that] of the Federal ALP cannot be a member of the FPLP.[136]

The effect of Scullin's ruling meant that as Ward was elected on a Lang Labor ticket, he was duly excluded from Caucus. Scullin's ruling immediately lead to a walk out of Beasley, Ward, Lazzarini, Eldridge, Dunn and Rae and this group formed the Lang Labor group. On 13 March, a day after the Lang group split from the party, at the conclusion of debate on the censure motion against the Government, Lyons crossed the floor with Fenton, Gabb, Guy and Jack Price to vote against Scullin and the Government as they were convinced that Theodore's financial plan would be ruinous to the country. The Government was now operating in a minority capacity with the Lang group holding the balance of power. On 27 March a Special Federal Conference was held to discuss the ramifications of the Lang Plan and the tumult that it had caused the party. At the opening of the Conference the President J.J Keneally stated:

> The conference was one of the most important in the history of the Labor Movement. It is a Special Conference, called to deal with a serious position that has arisen: a position which challenges the continuance of the Australian

---

[134] ibid.
[135] McMullin, 1991, op cit., p.170.
[136] *Caucus Minutes*, 12 March 1931.

Labor Party.[137]

The Conference duly passed a resolution declaring itself and the party firmly against Lang Labor stating:

> This conference declares against the Lang pronouncement to deliberately refuse to pay the interest obligation on loans raised from the general public in Australia and in England, which is contrary to Labor policy. Such action will not restore stable economic conditions and place men back at work; but on the contrary, will aggravate the position. Moreover, its application with respect to overseas debts would result inevitably in trade reprisals against Australia, and in other ways would lead to financial chaos and increased unemployment among our people.[138]

The resolution was particularly hollow given the already parlous state of the economy but it served its purpose to rally what was left of Labor behind its legislative program to enact the Theodore Plan with *The Worker* commenting:

> The Federal Labor Conference, sitting in Sydney, declared itself opposed to what is known as the 'Lang Plan' ... The Lang Plan is not a plan at all. On the contrary, it denotes the absence of a plan.
>
> ... The economic problems of Australia cannot be solved by such crude methods. We have got to nationalise banking. We have got to put a stop to borrowing by taking control of the whole monetary system of the Commonwealth and issuing all the credits needed for the development of the country.[139]

---

[137] Australian Labor Party, <u>Special Federal Conference</u>, Sydney, 27 March 1931, Sydney, p.2.
[138] <u>ibid.</u>, p.9.

The *Worker's* call for bank nationalisation in line with plank 4(a) of the Methods section of the platform was further indicative of the wider labour movement's position with respect to Labor calling a double dissolution and getting on with the job of governing the country and pursuing the platform.

Commonwealth Bank

The nationalisation of banking was a far cry from Labor's official financial plan that revolved around three Bills, the Fiduciary Notes Bill 1931; the Bank Interest Bill 1931 and the Commonwealth Bank Bill (No.2) 1931. The Bank Interest Bill sought to provide the Treasurer with absolute authority to vary rates of bank interest and discount. The Bill also sought to establish a Bank Interest Board to advise the Treasurer on the setting of rates, the Treasurer however would have absolute discretion to accept or reject the new Board's advice.[140] The Commonwealth Bank Bill (No.2) proposed that the Treasurer have the power to export the Commonwealth Bank's gold holdings to meet the Commonwealth Government's overseas debts thus effectively removing Australia from the gold standard. The note issue, instead of being fixed to the gold standard would be fixed to a proposed fiduciary note issue. The proposal was exceedingly bold, and was viewed by Sawer as:

> ... a simple act of desperation to meet an emergency situation.[141]

The pivotal Bill of the three was the Fiduciary Notes Bill, for without this Bill the other two could not stand alone. On 2 March Caucus approved of the Fiduciary Notes Bill being introduced into the Parliament and on 17 March Theodore outlined the Bill to the

---

[139] *The Worker*, 1 April 1931.
[140] For a copy of Theodore's second reading speech see; *C.P.D.*, Vol. 28, 25 March 1931, pp.571-7.
[141] Sawer, op cit., p.15.

House:

> The Bill provides for a fiduciary currency. The notes printed by authority of this measure will be known as treasury notes. An amount not exceeding £18,000,000 will be issued by the Commonwealth Bank Board. Of that amount a sum not exceeding £6,000,000 will be issued, as and when required by the Governor General, for the purpose of providing relief to wheat growers ... There will also be an issue to an amount not exceeding £12,000,000 and not exceeding £1,000,000 in each month, to be issued as and when required by the Governor General for the purpose of providing employment on reproductive works.[142]

The Government's proposals caused a furore:

> ... [and] outside Parliament the public debate on the Bill raged furiously. For some weeks the conservative press printed illustrations of bank notes and postage stamps, of enormous face values, which had to be used during the ruinous German inflation of the 1920s.[143]

Gibson had also been applying his own unique brand of pressure on the Government. On 11 March Theodore had written to Gibson requesting the Bank to release sufficient funds for the relief of wheat growers and the unemployed:

> The Commonwealth Bank ... make advances to the Commonwealth Government as and when required, up to a total of £3,500,00 to enable the whole scheme of relief to wheat growers to operate at once. I have to request further that an advance of £1,000,000 to be made at once to the

---

[142] *C.P.D.*, Vol. 128, 17 March 1931, p.300.
[143] Robertson, <u>op cit.</u>, p.332.

Commonwealth Government for the relief of unemployment.[144]

Labor's focus was on alleviating the plight of the destitute and the unemployed, any thought of realistically pursuing the platform had long since evaporated, Gibson responded on 2 April in his capacity as Chairman of the Loan Council informing Theodore:

> It was the unpleasant duty of the Board to advise the Loan Council that a point being reached beyond which it would be impossible for the bank to provide further financial assistance for the government.[145]

Gibson had shown that he was not willing to listen to the Government and instead threatened it with bankruptcy. With Gibson's threat still ringing in his ears, Scullin warned the Senate that if it [the Fiduciary Notes Bill] was lost 'in another place', a double dissolution election would be called.[146] On 17 April the Bill was defeated on the second reading in the Senate and when the Bill returned to the House Scullin stated:

> I say definitely that the Bill which the Senate has rejected will be sent back to it at the earliest possible moment that it can be sent under the Constitution, and if it is rejected we shall go to the country.[147]

Scullin's rhetoric was sharp, however the Bill was never submitted to the Senate and the Bank Interest Bill was also abandoned. Scullin had brought Labor to the brink of a double dissolution and again retreated, however Labor continued to proceed with the Commonwealth Bank Bill (No.2) in the forlorn hope that the

---

[144] Schedvin, op cit., p.241.
[145] Robertson, op cit., p.334.
[146] *Argus*, 8 April 1931.
[147] *C.P.D.*, Vol. 128, 17 April 1931, p.987.

Senate would pass it.

On 27 April, the Government was facing a critical situation of a possible default on a short term loan due on 30 June, Scullin spoke about the necessity to pass the Bill:

> Our proposals have been fought bitterly in the House of Representatives and thrown out by the Senate without any alternative having been offered. Relief for the unemployed and the wheatgrowers is urgent and vital. Nothing except a tax on bread is offered in place of measures for relief. On 30 June Treasury Bills amounting to £5,000,000 fall due in London. The Commonwealth Bank Board has written informing the Ministry that it can give no assistance to meet this obligation. The loan market is closed, and the Commonwealth Bank is helpless. The only recourse left is to ship gold to London at once, otherwise Australia will default in nine weeks' time.[148]

Scullin's dire assessment of the Government's financial predicament had little impact on the Opposition and on 7 May Latham resigned from his position as Leader of the Opposition and Labor's ex Treasurer Lyons took control of the Opposition and formed the United Australia Party,[149] with the Melbourne *Age* commenting:

> The United Australia Movement has numerous component parts. In it ultra-Labor elements and ultra-Conservative elements meet … Mr Lyons explained that they want a movement free from party politics.[150]

Lyons told Australia that he would lead a Party free from party

---

148 *Argus*, 28 April 1931.
149 *C.P.D.*, Vol.129, 7 May 1931, pp.1690-1.
150 The *Age*, Melbourne, 7 May 1931.

politics and in his first act as leader of this new 'movement' he led a party political censure motion against his old comrades. A week later on 13 May Lyons' Party rejected Scullin's Commonwealth Bank Bill (No.2) in the Senate and in an ironic twist of fate it was Lyons who effectively killed off the Theodore Plan, as it was Theodore's re-inclusion to Cabinet, at Scullin's request, that led to Lyons leaving Labor in the first place. Scullin was left with two realistic options. First, he had an opportunity to pursue the Fiduciary Notes Bill to a double dissolution, but for all his previous rhetoric about undertaking such action he backed away from his threat to go to the people. Second, in order to prolong the tenure of the government he would have to compromise with the Opposition to the extent that the basic tenets of the Melbourne Agreement be implemented. Scullin had rejected the first option, and rather than default on Government Loans he proceeded with the second.

In the period that Labor had been attempting to implement the Theodore Plan, Gibson had been busy behind the scenes attempting to establish a forum for State Premiers to discuss the financial and economic condition of the country and when Labor's legislation was again crushed by the Senate he suggested that a Premiers' Conference be convened to discuss implementing policies in line with the Melbourne Agreement. Scullin and Theodore attended the Conference that lasted from 25 May to 10 June, the outcome of which comprised three main elements:

1. The reduction of 20 percent of adjustable government expenditure (with the exception that old age pensions were only to be reduced by 12.5%). The total saving under this heading was expected to be £12,000,000.
2. Increases in Commonwealth income and sales tax, and primage duties. These increases were estimated to yield £7,500,000. In addition, increased state income tax was

suggested, although this did not form a specific part of the plan. An extra £2,000,000 could, it was thought, be raised under this heading.

3. The reduction of public and private interest rates. The conversion loan, which would involve reduction at the rate of 22.5%, would involve a saving of £5,500,000. Bank interest was to be reduced by voluntary action, mortgage rates by state legislation, and also rents (although these were not referred to specifically in the plan). The reduction in private interest rates was to conform to the 20% standard.[151]

Scullin approved what became known as the 'Premiers' Plan' and on 11 June he took it to Caucus for ratification. It should have been no surprise to Scullin that Caucus was shocked at what he proposed, with Lacey moving that:

> We [Caucus] do not approve of any reduction of Old Age Pensions, Invalid or War pensions; neither do we approve of any scheme which does not provide for adequate provision to employ the unemployed and make provision for necessitous farmers but suggest that other avenues be exploited with a view to savings being effected, especially in regard to the duplication of Parliaments etc.[152]

Scullin ruled Lacey's motion out of order and in the subsequent vote the Caucus approved the Premiers' Plan by twenty-six votes to thirteen. The fallout from the adoption of the Premiers' Plan was almost immediate with Holloway resigning from Caucus the next day because of the harsh cuts to pensions and Culley followed Holloway two weeks later for the same reason.[153] According to

---

[151] Report of the Sub-Committee of the Australian Loan Council',
Commonwealth Parliamentary Papers 1929-1931, Vol.II, 23 May 1931, pp.351-3.
[152] *Caucus Minutes*, 11 June 1931.
[153] Holloway and Culley were both senior members of their respective Trades

Schedvin there were three specific factors that helped create the conditions for the adoption of the Premiers' Plan:

1. The large Opposition majority in the Senate which thwarted government measures on every possible occasion. As it was unable to implement its own policy and unwilling to face a general election, the government had little alternative than to acquiesce in a compromise which was heavily weighted in favour of its political opponents. Indeed, on financial matters the Senate followed the Bank's line to an extent which suggests that it acted as Sir Robert Gibson's political arm.

2. The disintegration of the Labor Party and with it the government. The government knew full well that fragmentation meant political annihilation and that an approach to the electorate on its economic policy could not be considered seriously. Knowing the government's political weakness, the Bank and the Senate could increase pressure on it without fear of reprisal.

3. The influence of the economists. Their report made compromise possible because it had the appearance of expertise and objectivity. In fact, however, the report was carefully framed so as to be acceptable to both parties: one side was offered wage cuts and the other a reduction in interest rates. The economists of their own volition had little influence on the broad principles of the plan; these were determined for them by political exigencies. Nevertheless, the important part they played in providing the framework for a workable compromise should not be underestimated. None of

---

Hall Councils and were unable to accept the implementation of the Premiers' Plan.

these factors can, however, compare with the influence of the Commonwealth Bank; indeed two of the three were largely conditioned by Bank policy. It remains, therefore, that the Premiers' Plan was in conception and design, if not in execution, the Bank's plan.[154]

Gibson was the architect and driving force behind the Premiers' Plan, and Scullin accepted his financial prescription, a prescription that was the antithesis to Labor's platform and all Labor had fought against since its election. During the remainder of the fourth session and all through the fifth session[155] of Parliament Labor existed on a day to day basis.

The Demise of the Scullin Government

During the fifth session Labor successfully passed fifteen Acts, however none of these was remotely related to the platform, and instead the major impact of the legislation in the final period of Scullin's administration was geared towards implementing the Premiers' Plan. Commonwealth *Debt Conversion* and *Debt Conversion Agreement Acts*[156] and *Financial Emergency Acts*[157] took precedence in the Parliament. On 18 June Lazzarini summed up Labor's policy agenda to enact the Premiers' Plan in a debate on the first Debt Conversion Agreement Bill stating:

> This is not a Labor policy that has been put before the House – it is merely something that will make the reactionary forces of the country laugh. It cuts right across the idealism, the principles, and the philosophy of Labor … If it can be described as the policy of Labor, I say to the

---

[154] Schedvin, op cit., p.252-3.

[155] See; *C.P.D.*, Vol. 132, 16 September – 26 November 1931.

[156] *Commonwealth Debt Conversion Act* 1931; *Debt Conversion Act* 1931; *Commonwealth Debt Conversion Act (No.2)* 1931 and the *Debt Conversion Agreement Act* 1931.

[157] *Financial Emergency Act* 1931 and the *Financial Emergency Act (No.2)* 1931

men and women who are members of our industrial
organisations, who have made sacrifices and fought
strenuously for the cause of Labor for 40 years, look after
your gardens and your own affairs, let Labor alone; it is no
longer of any use to you. I urge them not to support a
policy that jettisons every ideal of Labor ... if these
proposals are accepted every vestige of the Labor policy will
be destroyed.[158]

The Government enacted the Premiers' Plan and in doing so
placed further hardship and misery on the backs of the people that,
through the enactment of its platform, it was pledged to protect.
The argument that it was better for Labor to enact the Premiers'
Plan rather than the Opposition in government held no merit and
Anstey summed up the situation best:

This is the annihilation of everything that the Labor Party
has produced during two long generations ... This
government has, since it took office, pursued a policy of
drift. It has suffered ignominy upon ignominy ... But are
we justified is spitting upon the altar of Labor simply
because others may desecrate it worse than we may? ...
That is not the path of salvation ... this Government is
crucifying the very people who raised its members from
obscurity and placed them in power.[159]

The *Sydney Morning Herald* was quick to report on Anstey's attack on
his own party, however the most poignant aspect of the report was
that it provided an insight into the depth of feeling and emotion
that this measure had generated within the government:

The interest aroused by the oratory of Mr Hughes was mild

---

[158] *C.P.D.*, Vol. 128, 18 June 1931, pp.2802-3.
[159] *C.P.D.*, Vol. 128, 8 July 1931, pp.3563-5.

compared with the excitement created by Mr Anstey, when thrill followed thrill in quick succession. The member for Bourke can make the pulses of his hearers surge by the sheer force and passion of his language. He flogged those who supported the plan with a scourge of hard and bitter words and added to the wounds the salt of a stinging ridicule, and, mingling irony with sarcasm, he reviewed the history of the Scullin administration and left it without a tatter of political reputation. He said 'This Labor Government has outraged every principle it was sworn to preserve and been false to the class that had given it its life'.[160]

The Government remained in power until 25 November when Beasley moved the adjournment debate in the House on the Unemployment Relief Grant charging Theodore and the Government with impropriety in the way that it handled the administration of the grant.[161] Theodore denied any impropriety,[162] however in the subsequent division the Government was defeated by thirty-seven votes to thirty-two when the Lang Labor group crossed the floor. The *Labor Call* likened Beasley's crossing of the floor as 'bovine stupidity',[163] whilst the *Worker* labelled the Beasley group, 'traitors to Labor'.[164] On 26 November Scullin addressed the House:

> In consequence of the vote carried yesterday, I waited on the Governor General this morning and tendered him the advice contained in the following letter:
>
>> I beg to inform you that yesterday a motion for the adjournment of the House was carried against the

---

[160] *Sydney Morning Herald*, 9 July 1931.
[161] *C.P.D.*, Vol 132, 25 November 1931, pp.1888-92.
[162] ibid., pp.1892-4.
[163] *Labor Call*, 3 December 1931.
[164] *Worker* (Brisbane), 2 December 1931.

> government, by a majority of five, by a combination of the Nationalist party, the Country Party, and the group led by Mr Beasley. I formally advise Your Excellency to grant a dissolution of the House of Representatives.[165]

The general election was announced for 19 December and Labor was slaughtered at the ensuing poll. Labor's first preference vote plunged to just 27.09% and it only won thirteen out of seventy-five seats in the House, and in the Senate Labor numbers dropped to just eight.[166] The loss was particularly galling for a large section of the labour movement who laid the blame for the loss at the feet of Lang, the conservative parties and the hostile press, with *The Worker* stating:

> The Federal Labor Government was defeated last Saturday, not because it had fallen down on the job of governing the country during a crisis unprecedented in the history of the Commonwealth, but because the electors were stampeded by the vile and unscrupulous propaganda campaign launched by the anti-Labor forces and the base treachery of the Lang Faction Party ... For sheer political dirtiness and barefaced misrepresentation the campaign launched ... by the Sydney Daily Telegraph would be hard to beat.[167]

The Worker was adamant about why Labor was defeated and who was to blame for the defeat, however Scullin was philosophical when questioned about Labor's performance:

> Defeat is the fate of a government, which has had the

---

165 *C.P.D.*, Vol 132, 26 November 1931, p.1926
166 For an analysis of the 1931 election see; Sawer, <u>op cit</u>., p.42-3; and McMullin, 1991, <u>op cit</u>., p.177-80 and Robertson, <u>op cit</u>., pp.362-79,
167 *The Worker*, 23 December 1931.

responsibility of governing the nation during a financial crisis ... My personal regrets are at the loss of earnest and able colleagues, and at the disappointment of strong supporters who have never wavered in their allegiance to the Government. However, the people have spoken, and theirs is the deciding voice.[168]

---

[168] *Argus*, 21 December 1931.

5 CONCLUSION

Scullin's analysis of Labor's performance highlighted the Depression as the major reason for the loss. It is undeniable that the Depression was a major determinant in Labor's inability to enact the platform in a similar capacity to Fisher from 1910 to 1913. Also, another major obstacle that Scullin had to contend with that was absent during Fisher's administration was Labor's inability to have its legislation pass the Senate without it either being slaughtered or heavily amended so that the end product had no resemblance to that which was initially introduced. In reflecting on Labor's legislative achievements vis-à-vis enacting the platform Sawer stated:

> … little of this legislation derived from the election policy of the ALP, still less its long term program.[169]

Sawer was of the view that the Government's inability to legislate for the platform was based on two separate but interrelated factors:

> The Government was hag-ridden by the economic crisis, and by the hostile Senate, which together forced it into measures designed mainly by its opponents, and anathema to most of its followers; these measures were designed to spread the burden of the economic crisis 'equitably' – that is, so as to preserve a substantially private-enterprise

---

[169] Sawer, op cit., p.10.

economy with about the same relative class distribution of income and capital as obtained before the crisis occurred. Hence the chief legislative monument to the government was the series of financial measures enforcing reductions in salaries, wages, pensions and social services, and inviting and in the finish enforcing reductions in interest payments on the public debt.[170]

Sawer's analysis is poignant, however it should be noted that whilst the economic conditions of the time were egregious and the Senate overtly hostile and often destructive in its handling of Labor's legislative program, Scullin had two excellent opportunities to address the political situation in the Senate by forcing a double dissolution election that could have gifted Labor control of the Senate. However, neither opportunity was pursued and this coupled with the fact that Scullin chose to be out of the country during crucial times during his administration only added to his government's problems that eventually brought about Labor's demise at the polls in 1931.

The Scullin Labor Government was severely restricted in its ability to successfully enact the platform and it was forced to enact a legislative program largely in keeping with its Opponents' policy initiatives rather than its own platform. However, despite this fact a wholesale critique of the administration's shortcomings should be viewed cautiously. Labor, once again came to office at a time of great international unrest, except this time it did not face a world war it had to manage during a period of global economic and financial crisis and depression. Labor formed a Government after thirteen years' in the political wilderness and had to contend with a global economic and financial crisis the likes of which the world had never experienced, as well as dealing with a recalcitrant Senate

---

[170] ibid.

that mauled nearly every piece of legislation that was submitted to it. Also, the obdurate Chair of the Commonwealth Bank was an individual who did everything in his power to make life a misery for the Labor administration battling to keep its head above water.

Labor's first six months in office were relatively uneventful in respect of pursuing the platform, however Labor moved to strengthen plank 2 of the 'Finance and Taxation' section of the platform by passing legislation related to Land Taxes. This measure was hardly ground breaking, however it was a positive step in the right direction. Labor was under no illusion as to the enormity of the task it faced, even if it did not fully comprehend the enormity of the tidal wave that was about to engulf it. Labor did not control the Senate but this did not stop it pursuing key platform planks by introducing three separate pieces of legislation to alter the Constitution. Labor was aware of the policy agenda it wished to pursue and did not hesitate on passing three Constitution Alteration Bills through the House. The Bills, if passed through the Senate and at a Referendum would have provided Labor with the power to amend the Constitution by obtaining a clear majority in both Houses, as well as expanding the powers of the federal government in the fields of industrial arbitration and trade and commerce. The Bills pursued key planks of the platform but were killed off in the Senate. Scullin then had an opportunity to force a double dissolution, and after threatening to do so, he withdrew the Bills from the government program. The defeat of the referenda proposals was a blow to Labor and not entirely unexpected. However, undaunted the Government then actively pursued key platform planks including the establishment of a Central Reserve Bank, the introduction of Conciliation and Arbitration legislation and legislation to establish cooperative wide pools for wheat and hops. In April 1930, Labor introduced the Wheat Marketing Bill and the Hops Marketing Bill in line with sub plank 10 of the 'National Work' section of the platform, the Bills were passed through the House where Labor controlled the chamber but were dismantled in the Senate. In May 1930, Labor introduced the Central Reserve Bank Bill in line with plank 1 of the 'Finance and Taxation' section of the platform that called on Labor to establish a Central Reserve Bank. Again, the Bill passed through the House but was effectively rendered useless and finally killed off in the Senate. Also, in May 1930 Labor introduced the Conciliation and Arbitration Bill to strengthen the existing industrial reform planks of the platform, but again the Bill passed through the House only to be defeated in the Senate.

An analysis of the Bills introduced into the Parliament show that the Scullin Government attempted to enact key planks of the platform, including legislation on banking reform, industrial relations, national work, land taxes and constitutional initiatives, all of which were successfully passed through the House but were put to the sword in the Senate. There is little doubt that Labor was overwhelmed by the sheer magnitude of the crisis which they faced, a crisis that ultimately decimated the party at the federal election in 1931. However, what is also clear is that Labor did pursue the platform and but for the Senate would have enacted a number of its key platform planks.

6 APPENDICES

APPENDIX 1 - OFFICIAL FEDERAL PARLIAMENTARY LABOR PARTY PLATFORM 1927

OBJECTIVE

The Socialisation of Industry, Production and Exchange.

METHODS

Socialisation of Industry by –

(a) The constitutional utilisation of the Federal, State and Municipal Government Parliamentary and administrative machinery;

(b) The extension of the scope and powers of the Commonwealth Bank until complete control of banking is in the hands of the people;

(c) The organisation and establishment of co-operative activities, in which the workers and other producers shall be trained in the management, responsibility and control of industry;

(d)   The cultivation of Labor ideals and principles and the development of the spirit of social service;

(e) The setting up of Labor research and Labor information bureaux and of Labor educational institutions;

(f) Progressive enactment of reform as defined in the Labor Platform.

FIGHTING PLATFORM

1. The cultivation of an Australian sentiment, the maintenance of a White Australia and the development in Australia of an enlightened and self-reliant community.

2.

    (a) Complete self-Government for Australia as a Member of the British Commonwealth of Nations.

    (b) No Imperial Federation.

    (c) Unlimited legislative powers for the Commonwealth Parliament and such delegated powers to the States or Provinces as the Commonwealth Parliament may determine from time to time.

3. Nationalisation of Banking and Insurance.

4. Nationalisation of Monopolies.

5. Arbitration Act Amendment to include –

    (a) The establishment of a maximum 44 hour week throughout Australia, with special provisions where health is menaced and for women workers.

    (b) Standard of living not inferior to the basis of the Piddington Basic Wage Commission finding.

6. Navigation Laws.

7. Commonwealth Freight and Passenger Steamers.

8. Restriction of Public Borrowing.

9. Electoral Reform.

10. Initiative and Referendum.

11. Abolition of State Legislative Councils.

12. Abolition of State Governors.

13. Abolition of Senate.

14. Amending Workers' Compensation Act.

15. National Monopoly of Assurance, including sick, accident, life and unemployment.

16. Motherhood and Childhood Endowment.

17. Amendment of Defence Act.

CONSTITUTION AND ELECTORAL REFORM

1. Complete Self Government for Australia as a Member of the British Commonwealth of Nations. No Imperial Federation. Administration on advice of Australian Ministers only, subject to the control of the Commonwealth Parliament. All legislation, except such as appears inconsistent with Ministers only. No further Imperial honors to be granted in any circumstances to Australian citizens.

The Commonwealth Constitution to be amended to provide:

(a) Unlimited legislative powers for the Commonwealth Parliament, and such delegated powers to the States or provinces as the Commonwealth Parliament may determine from time to time.

(b) The Commonwealth Parliament to be vested with authority to create new states and provinces.

(c) The Senate to be abolished.

(d) The High Court of Australia to have final jurisdiction in all Australian causes.

(e) The principle of adult suffrage to be embodied in the Constitution.

(f) The initiative, referendum and recall.

2. Maintenance of a White Australia

3. Adult Suffrage to be made part of the Commonwealth Constitution.

4. Amendment of the Electoral Act to provide for compulsory voting.

5. Initiative, Referendum and Recall.

6. Abolition of State Legislative Councils.

7. Abolition of State Governors.

8. Abolition of Senate.

9. Alteration of Constitution to give authority to Commonwealth Government to proceed (if necessary without concurrence of the States, provided the Commonwealth Government furnishes the money) to the unification of the railway gauges in accordance with the scheme laid down by the Royal Commission.

10. The Commonwealth Electoral Act to be amended so as to remove the existing disqualification against State members contesting Federal seats and the Senate.

FINANCE AND TAXATION REFORM

1. The Commonwealth Bank to be developed on the lines of a Central Reserve Bank, while retaining its ordinary and Savings-Bank functions. Its operations to be extended to give greater assistance to the primary and other industries of the country. The Commonwealth Bank to remain, in the matter of policy, free from association or agreement with the private banks.

2.

   (a) Maintenance of Graduated Tax on Unimproved Land Values, where estates are over 5000 in value.

   (b) Amendment of existing Land Tax Act to provide that the graduation shall not apply to the different portions of the values of large estates. That the maximum of the tax be not less than 1/- in the pound, while maintaining the present exemption of 5000.

3. Naval and military expenditure to be allotted from the proceeds of direct taxation.

4. The New Protection, embodying effective protection of Australian industries, prevention of profiteering and the protection of the workers in such industries.

5. Import embargoes for the effective protection of Australian industries, subject to the control of prices and industrial conditions in the industry benefited.

6. Restriction of Public Borrowing.

7. Income Tax – All incomes from personal exertion of not less than 300 to be exempt from Income Tax, with a further deduction from the taxable income of 100 for a taxpayer's wife and 60 for each child and others wholly dependent on the taxpayer.

8. Until the Constitution is amended in accordance with Plank 1 of the General Platform, the per capita payments to the states to be continued without diminution.

9. No additional preference to the United Kingdom or any other country except under an equitable reciprocal arrangement.

INDUSTRIAL REFORM

1. Amendment of Workers' Compensation Act to provide compensation for sufferers from industrial disease (such as miners' phthisis), and the securing of adequate benefits for injured or disabled workers, the scheme to be based on the compulsory assurance of all workers.

2. Commonwealth Mines and Regulation Act.

3. The Commonwealth Conciliation and Arbitration Act be amended to provide:

(a)   Appeals as of right to the High Court against decision of State Civil Courts relating to the interpretation of Federal Awards.

(b)   Representatives of employers and employees to have right to check data on which Commonwealth Statistician's figures are based.

(c)   Power to declare a Common Rule.

4. That Provision be made to establish a Board on similar lines to that of the British Board of Trade, vested with power to investigate all serious railway accidents occurring on the railways and other forms of transport, and to make and enforce regulations governing those engaged in and in charge of transport operations throughout Australia. That provision be made for the industrial side to be represented by representatives of the employees apart from those of the administrative staffs.

SOCIAL REFORM

1. Civil Equality of Men and Women.

2. Uniform laws of Marriage and Divorce.

3. Widows' and Children's Pensions.

4. Increased Old Age and Invalid Pensions.

5. Motherhood and Childhood Endowment.

6. Abolition of Capital Punishment and Flogging.

NATIONAL WORK

1. Nationalisation of Banking and Insurance.

2. Nationalisation of Monopolies.

3. Commonwealth Sugar Refinery.

4. Nationalisation of Shipping.

5. National Assurance, including Sick, Accident, Life and Unemployment.

6. Nationalisation of Public Health.

7. Development of commercial aviation.

8. Government control of wireless.

9. Development and settlement of Northern Australia.

10. Australian wide co-operative pools for the marketing and financing of farm products.

11. Extension of the Commonwealth Shipping Line. The line to be kept independent of the Shipping Combine.

12. Subsidising of secondary industries on a co-operative basis.

NAVIGATION

1. Navigation laws to provide -

  (a) For the protection of Australian shipping against unfair competition.

  (b) Registration of all vessels engaged in the coastal trade.

  (c) The efficient manning of vessels.

  (d) The proper supply of life saving and other equipment.

(e) The regulation of hours and conditions of work.

(f) Proper accommodation for passengers and seamen.

(g) Proper loading gear and inspection of same.

(h) Compulsory insurance of crews by shipowners against accident or death.

(i) That the Plimsoll mark, which was suspended during the war, be restored on all ships as it was before the war.

DEFENCE

1. Adequate home defence against possible foreign aggression.

2. That the Commonwealth Constitution be amended to include a condition that no Australian can be conscripted for military service.

3. Amendment of Defence Act to secure –

   (a) Deletion of all clauses relating to compulsory training and service;

   (b) Any sentence imposed by court martial to be subject to review by a civil court;

   (c) No offence to be created by regulation; no penalty to be imposed by regulation;

   (d) No employment of or interference by soldiers in industrial disputes;

   (e) No raising of forces for service outside the Commonwealth or participation or promise of participation in any future overseas war, except by decision of the people.

REPATRIATION

1. Liberal treatment to be extended to all soldiers disabled as a result of war service and their dependents. Creation of an Appeal Board to finally decide all appeals relating to war pensions.

2. Sympathetic administration of Repatriation in relation to the valuation and terms of conditions of occupancy of farm properties and homes provided for returned soldiers and their dependents.

IMMIGRATION

Immigration to be strictly regulated and linked with Land Settlement and the expansion of Secondary Industries.

(Note – An influx of Immigrants in circumstances that would imperil Australian Industrial conditions, by over competition for the work available, would not be approved. The Labor Party's policy is designed to create further employment for the people already here and opportunities for new-comers by the breaking up of large estates and the expansion of primary and secondary industries.

To protect Australian workers, Immigration schemes must be carefully controlled and unemployment Insurance provided.)

APPENDIX 2 – SCULLIN'S CONSTITUTION ALTERATION PROPOSALS

<u>A Bill for an Act</u>

To alter the constitution by conferring upon the Parliament full power to amend the constitution.

Be it enacted by the King's Most Excellent Majesty, the Senate, and the House of Representatives of the Commonwealth of Australia, with the approval of the electors, as required by the constitution, as follows:

1. This Act may be cited as the Constitution Alteration (Power of Amendment) 1930.

2. The Constitution is altered by inserting, after section one hundred and twenty-eight, the following section:

    '129.   Notwithstanding anything in the last preceding section, the Parliament shall have full power to alter the Constitution in the following manner:

    The proposed law for the alteration thereof shall, after the lapse of one month from its origination in a House of the Parliament, be passed by an absolute majority of each House of the Parliament, and be assented to by the Governor-General.'[171]

The second measure was the Constitution Alteration (Industrial Powers) Bill that sought to extend the Government's power in the

---

[171] *Caucus Minutes*, 5 March 1930. (Note - section 2 of the Bill was amended by Caucus on 13 March 1930. The original section stated: *'128. This constitution shall not be altered except in the following manner: The proposed law for the alteration thereof must, after the lapse of one month from its origination in a House of the parliament, be passed by an absolute majority of each House of the Parliament, and must receive the Royal assent.'*

field of industrial relations in line with plank 5 of the fighting platform and planks 1 to 4 of the Industrial Reform section of the platform. Scullin provided the draft proposal to Caucus:

<u>A Bill for an Act</u>

To alter the provisions of the Constitution with respect to industrial matters.

Be it enacted by the King's Most Excellent Majesty, the Senate, and the House of Representatives of the Commonwealth of Australia, with the approval of the electors, as required by the constitution, as follows:

1. This Act may be cited as the Constitution Alteration (Industrial Power) 1930.

2. Section fifty-one of the constitution is altered by omitting from paragraph XXXV the words:

    (a) Labor

    (b) Employment and unemployment

    (c) Terms and conditions of labour and employment in any trade, industry, occupation or calling

    (d) The rights and obligations of employers and employees

    (e) Strikes and lock-outs

    (f) The maintenance of industrial peace; and

    (g) The settlement of industrial disputes.[172]

---

[172] <u>ibid.</u>

94

7 BIBLIOGRAPHY

Newspapers

Argus

Australian Worker

Labor Call

Labor Daily

Sydney Morning Herald

The Age

The Worker

Worker (Brisbane)

Government Publications

C.P.D., Vol. 121, 11 September 1929.

C.P.D., Vol. 121, 10 September 1929.

C.P.D., Vol. 122, 21 November 1929.

C.P.D., Vol. 122, 21 November 1929.

C.P.D., Vol.122, 21 November 1929.

C.P.D., Vol.122, 1929.

C.P.D., Vol. 123, 1930.

C.P.D., Vol. 123, 19 March 1930 and Senate, 20 March 1930.

C.P.D., Vol 123, 14 March 1930.

C.P.D., Vol. 123, 14 March 1930.

C.P.D., Vol. 123, 4 April 1930.

C.P.D., Vol. 123, 8 April 1930.

C.P.D., Vol. 125, 4 July 1930.

C.P.D., Vol. 123, 1 May 1930.

C.P.D., Vol 124, 28 May 1930.

C.P.D., Vol. 124, 30 May 1930.

C.P.D., Vol. 124, 30 May 1930,.

C.P.D., Vol. 124, 8 August 1930.

C.P.D., Vol. 127, 30 October – 18 December 1930.

C.P.D., Vol. 128, 6 March 1931.

C.P.D., Vol. 128, 12 March 1931.

C.P.D., Vol. 28, 25 March 1931.

C.P.D., Vol. 128, 17 March 1931.

C.P.D., Vol. 128, 17 April 1931.

C.P.D., Vol.129, 7 May 1931.

C.P.D., Vol. 132, 16 September – 26 November 1931.

C.P.D., Vol. 128, 18 June 1931.

C.P.D., Vol. 128, 8 July 1931.

C.P.D., Vol 132, 25 November 1931.

C.P.D., Vol 132, 26 November 1931.

Proceedings and Decisions of the Conference of Commonwealth and State Ministers. *Commonwealth Parliamentary Papers*, Vol. II, February 1931.

'Notes on the Economic Position of Australia, October 1929'. *Brigden Papers*, NLA, 21/5/163.

ALP Federal Conference Records

Australian Labor Party, <u>Official Report of Proceedings of the 12th Commonwealth Conference</u>, Canberra, 26-29 May 1930.

Australian Labor Party, <u>Special Federal Conference</u>, Sydney, 27 March 1931, Sydney.

ALP Federal Caucus Minutes

Caucus Minutes, 13 November 1929.

Caucus Minutes, 13 March 1930.

Caucus Minutes, 2 April 1930.

Caucus Minutes, 29 May 1930.

Caucus Minutes, 3 April 1930.

Caucus Minutes, 27 October 1930.

Caucus Minutes, 6 November 1930.

Caucus Minutes, 12 November 1930.

Caucus Minutes, 18 February 1931.

Caucus Minutes, 12 March 1931.

Caucus Minutes, 11 June 1931.

Books and Journal Articles

Barrett, R.H., (1963) Promises and Performances in Australian Politics 1928 – 1963. Publications Centre, University of British Columbia, Canada.

Crisp, L.F., (1977) Australian National Government. Longman Cheshire, Melbourne, Australia.

Holloway, E. J., From Labour Council to Privy Council. Unpublished Autobiography.

Kennedy. K., (1978) <u>The Mungana Affair</u>. University of Queensland Press, Brisbane.

McMullin, R., (1991) <u>The Light on the Hill: The Australian Labor Party 1891-1991</u>. Oxford University Press Australia.

Robertson, J., (1974) <u>J.H. Scullin. A Political Biography</u>. University Western Australia Press, Perth.

Ross,. (1977) <u>John Curtin a Biography</u>. MacMillan & Co. Australia.

Sawer, G., (1956) <u>Australian Federal Politics and Law 1901-1929</u>. Melbourne University Press.

Schedvin, C.B., (1970) <u>Australia and the Great Depression.</u> Sydney University Press.

Lonie, J., Good Labor Men: The Hill Government in South Australia, 1930-1933, *Labour History* 31, 1976.

Frank Anstey: Memoirs of the Scullin Labor Government, 1929-1932. *Historical Studies*, Vol. 18, No. 72, April 1979.

ABOUT THE AUTHOR

Dr John McSwiney holds degrees in Economics/Politics and Law, he has a Masters of Politics and a Doctorate of Philosophy from Monash University. John joined the Labor Party when he was 18 and won preselection for the Federal seat of Isaacs when he was 24 contesting the seat as part of Paul Keating's team at the 1993 Federal election. John has had careers in politics, law, government and international business. His roles have included being a Barrister and Solicitor of the Supreme Court of Victoria; the Director International Education, VCAA; CEO Haileybury International School, China; and Director, Technical Training (Eng.) Royal Australian Navy.

Scullin and the Great Depression